AID AND DEVELOPMENT

ABOUT THE AUTHOR

Myles Wickstead CBE is Visiting Professor (International Relations) at the Open University and at King's College, University of London. He has held senior positions in the UK Department for International Development (DFID) and Foreign and Commonwealth Office. He has been Head of the British Development Division in Eastern Africa; represented the UK on the Executive Board of the World Bank; served as British Ambassador to Ethiopia, Djibouti, and the African Union; and was Head of Secretariat to the Commission for Africa.

He is an adviser to 'Hand in Hand International' and 'Development Initiatives' and is on the Boards of a number of NGOs, trusts and foundations. He has been Chair of CONCERN UK and One World Media and Independent Vice-Chair of the Westminster Foundation for Democracy; and on the boards of the British Institute in Eastern Africa, the Crown Agents' Foundation, the Comic Relief International Grants Committee, and the Development Studies Association. He is currently on the boards of the Baring Foundation, the Joffe Charitable Trust, International Inspiration, Enterprise for Development, and the Advisory Council of Wilton Park, and is honorary Vice-President of Voluntary Service Overseas (VSO).

He is well-known as an international development practitioner and thinker, particularly on Africa, and has appeared regularly on radio and TV for programmes such as *Today*, *Hard Talk* and *The Moral Maze*. He has written extensively on Africa and development, contributing to a number of books, such as *Financing for Development*, (ed. Fratianni, Kirton and Savona; Ashgate, 2007) and *Networks of Influence*, (ed. Woods and Diaz; Oxford University Press, 2009).

Myles has degrees from the Universities of St Andrews (MA First Class Honours) and Oxford (MLitt), and has been awarded honorary doctorates by Leeds Metropolitan University, the Open University, and the University of Ulster in recognition of his work on Africa and development.

MYLES A. WICKSTEAD

AID AND DEVELOPMENT

A Brief Introduction

OXFORD
UNIVERSITY PRESS

OXFORD
UNIVERSITY PRESS

Great Clarendon Street, Oxford, OX2 6DP,
United Kingdom

Oxford University Press is a department of the University of Oxford.
It furthers the University's objective of excellence in research, scholarship,
and education by publishing worldwide. Oxford is a registered trade mark of
Oxford University Press in the UK and in certain other countries

© Myles A. Wickstead 2015

The moral rights of the author have been asserted

First Edition published in 2015

Impression: 1

Published in the United States of America by Oxford University Press
198 Madison Avenue, New York, NY 10016, United States of America

British Library Cataloguing in Publication Data
Data available

Library of Congress Control Number: 2015932985

ISBN 978-0-19-874492-4

Printed and bound by
CPI Group (UK) Ltd, Croydon, CR0 4YY

PREFACE

There is in truth no shortage of literature about aid and development. Much of it is excellent—but it generally presupposes a degree of practical engagement or specialized knowledge which many people interested in the subject do not yet have. There is perhaps room for a readily accessible and concise introduction, putting ideas about aid and development and their evolution into their historical and political context. This volume is designed to meet that need. It does not claim to be comprehensive; it aspires, after all, only to be 'A Brief Introduction'. Whilst it is not autobiographical or anecdotal, it is written mainly from a UK perspective and is largely based on my personal experience and engagement.

My hope is that the book will be of interest to international development academics and scholars, but at the same time be accessible to the general reader who would like to learn more about how aid and development have evolved over the past three-quarters of a century; the current state of the debate; and where aid and development might go next at a time of great flux in global economic and political relations. Inevitably, it is not possible to do more than skim the surface of some of the issues in a book of this sort; it will have done its job if it helps explain the overarching framework and stimulates the reader to dig deeper.

I have been particularly fortunate to have had a career which has spanned the UK Department for International Development (DFID)—and its predecessors—and the Foreign and Commonwealth Office, where I held some particularly interesting positions which have given me some of the insights on which this volume is based. These have included being private secretary to ministers in both departments; being responsible for UK development policy towards the EU in the aftermath of the fall of the Berlin Wall; running the UK regional Development Division based in East Africa in the mid-1990s; coordinating the 1997 UK Government White Paper *Eliminating World Poverty: A Challenge for the 21st Century* immediately after a new Labour government had been elected to office; and serving on the board of the World Bank (and as Development Counsellor at the British Embassy) in Washington from 1997 to 2000.

I was subsequently based in Addis Ababa as British Ambassador to Ethiopia, also covering Djibouti and the Organisation for African Unity as it transformed into the African Union. I returned to the UK at the beginning of 2004 as Head of Secretariat to the Commission for Africa, established by then Prime Minister Tony Blair. The Commission's Report *Our Common Interest* formed the basis of the G8 Gleneagles Summit communiqué on Africa the following year.

So there is a good deal in here about Africa and the international system, and a reasonable amount about Asia (and we should not forget the fact that there are still more very poor people in Asia than in Africa). There is very little about Latin America, or the dramatic and often violent shifts between left and right of Latin American countries, which seem at last to have moved into some sort of equilibrium. This is not a region that has had strong development links with the UK (though there were modest programmes in Bolivia and Peru in the 1970s). It also reflects the fact that there is in the western hemisphere only one country—Haiti, a historical victim of corrupt and tyrannical government, Cold War politics, and natural disasters—which is still classified as a 'least developed country'; a classification which will become crystal clear to those who persist to the end (or who go direct to the section on 'Developing Country Classifications' in Part Two).

Equally inevitably, the book reflects the perspective of a Western donor rather than that of—say—a civil society campaigner in the South. In 2015, there will at least be something approaching a common view between the two that the ultimate objective of aid and development is about improving the well-being of the poorest and most disadvantaged groups in less developed countries (even if that raises many questions—and fierce debate—about what poverty means, and how aid can best support that objective). It was not always thus, and what I have attempted to do is provide the historical context within which this welcome shift has been able to take place, and to offer some reflections on where it might all lead.

This book was largely drafted in 2014 and the beginning of 2015. For reasons which will I hope become evident, 2015 is a major year for aid and international development, and the book is intended to provide useful historical background to some of the discussions and debates which will take place in the second half of the year. By definition, there remains some uncertainty about the precise nature of the agreements that will be reached and the commitments that will be undertaken. Rather than waiting until those outcomes were certain, however, there seemed to be significant added value in charting now rather than later the process which has got us to this stage.

A number of people have provided help, advice, and comments as this book has been put together, and I am enormously grateful to them all. They include my academic colleagues Andy Summer and Mann Virdee at the International Development Institute, King's College London, and Richard Pinder and Behi Barzegar in Development Policy and Practice at the Open University. My colleagues at Development Initiatives (DI) Tim Strawson, Jenny Claydon, and Rebecca Hills have been enormously helpful in pointing me in the right direction on figures and statistics and to graphs and projections which are available on the Development Initiatives website <www.devinit.org> which I commend to readers of this volume. Lesley-Anne Long, Andrew Purkis, Michael Carter, and Kathryn Hingston, who have between them a formidable knowledge of particular institutions or aspects of development, have contributed a number of very helpful ideas and suggestions. I would like to thank Mike Wooldridge, Andy Sumner, and David Green for being prepared to stick their necks out and say some kind words about the book. Adam Swallow at Oxford

University Press has been a constant source of good advice and encouragement. I have been fortunate indeed to have my wife Shelagh and my children Edward and Kathryn alongside me sharing many of the experiences—and in particular living in Africa—on which this volume is based; and they were even prepared to look at the draft, which says something.

Despite all the wise advice and support from others, I do not suppose for one moment that this book is free from all errors of fact; for those of course I take full responsibility. No doubt readers will also find reason to take issue with some elements of judgement and interpretation; it would be disappointing were that not to be the case.

Myles A. Wickstead

May 2015

CONTENTS

CONTENTS

Part Two

LIST OF ABBREVIATIONS

ADB	Asian Development Bank
AFDB	African Development Bank
AIIB	Asia Infrastructure Investment Bank
APRM	Africa Peer Review Mechanism
ATT	arms trade treaty
AU	African Union
BMGF	Bill and Melinda Gates Foundation
BRICS	Brazil, Russia, India, China, and South Africa
BWIs	Bretton Woods institutions
CAP	Common Agricultural Policy
CBDR	common but differentiated responsibilities
CDF	Comprehensive Development Framework
CDI	Commitment to Development Index
CfA	Commission for Africa
CFTC	Commonwealth Fund for Technical Cooperation
CG	Consultative Group
CIFF	Children's Investment Fund Foundation
COMECON	Council for Mutual Economic Cooperation
CSO	Civil Society Organization
CSR	corporate social responsibility
DAC	Development Assistance Committee
DDR	disarmament, demobilization, and reintegration

DEC	Disasters Emergency Committee
EBRD	European Bank for Reconstruction and Development
ECOSOC	Economic and Social Council
EEC	European Economic Community
EPTA	Expanded Programme of Technical Assistance
ERP	Economic Recovery Programme
ERR	Economic Rate of Return
FAO	Food and Agriculture Organization
GATT	General Agreement on Tariffs and Trade
GAVI	Global Alliance on Vaccines and Immunizations
GMO	genetically modified organism
GPEDC	Global Partnership for Effective Development Cooperation
GPG	global public good
HIPC	Highly Indebted Poor Countries
HLM	High-Level Meeting
IADB	Inter-American Development Bank
IATI	International Aid Transparency Initiative
IBRD	International Bank for Reconstruction and Development
ICC	International Criminal Court
ICRC	International Committee of the Red Cross
ICSID	International Centre for Settlement of Investment Disputes
IDA	International Development Association
IFC	International Finance Corporation
IMF	International Monetary Fund
IDT	International Development Target

INGO	international non-governmental organization
LDC	least developed country
LEDC	less economically developed country
LIC	low income country
MDB	Multilateral Development Bank
MDG	Millennium Development Goal
MDRI	Multilateral Debt Relief Initiative
MIC	middle income country
MIGA	Multilateral Investment Guarantee Agency
MPH	Make Poverty History
NATO	North Atlantic Treaty Organization
NEPAD	New Partnership for Africa's Development
NGO	non-governmental organization
NIC	Newly Industrialized Country
NIEO	New International Economic Order
OVI	Objectively Verifiable Indicator
ODA	official development assistance
OECD	Organisation for Economic Cooperation and Development
OEEC	Organisation for European Economic Cooperation
OIOS	Office of Internal Oversight Services
OOF	Other Official Flows
OPEC	Organization of the Petroleum Exporting Countries
OSI	Open Society Institute
PCD	Policy Coherence for Development
PFP	Policy Framework Paper
PIU	Project Implementation Unit
PRSP	Poverty Reduction Strategy Paper

RDB	Regional Development Bank
SAP	structural adjustment programme
SDG	sustainable development goal
SDR	Special Drawing Right
SSR	Security Sector Reform
UNCTAD	United Nations Conference on Trade and Development
UNDG	United Nations Development Group
UNDP	United Nations Development Programme
UNEP	United Nations Environment Programme
UNESCO	United Nations Educational, Scientific and Cultural Organization
UNFPA	United Nations Fund for Population Activities
UNHCR	United Nations High Commissioner for Refugees
UNICEF	United Nations Children's Fund
UNOCHA	United Nations Office for the Coordination of Humanitarian Affairs
USSR	Union of Soviet Socialist Republics
WFP	World Food Programme
WHO	World Health Organization
WTO	World Trade Organization

INTRODUCTION

'Development' is what happens when human beings group themselves together in order to carry out a common endeavour for their mutual benefit, and to share the benefits of individual learning. The word 'development'—whether of individuals, institutions or nations—carries with it a sense of evolution, of bringing out latent capabilities through progressive stages towards a more rounded and complete entity. The word may sometimes be qualified by an adjective making it clear that it is in a particular case undesirable—an 'unwelcome development', for example, or an 'ugly housing development'—but generally it is positive and forward-looking.

Those European countries considered as the most developed in the eighteenth and nineteenth centuries were those which were able to achieve steady economic growth, which usually had its roots in a transformation from an agricultural-based to an industrial-based society. This in turn depended on major technical advances allowing for the more efficient exploitation of natural resources and the development of large-scale manufacturing industries; and the development of overseas posts and colonies which not only reflected those countries' struggle for political dominance in Europe but were also able to support their trading activities and supply the raw materials on which they depended.

In practice, for many people in Europe this new paradigm of development, driven by the industrial revolution, simply meant exchanging a life of rural poverty for a life of urban poverty, with the main benefits of economic growth, mechanization, and trade being enjoyed by an elite minority. Increasingly, however, even if its over-arching goal remained capital accumulation, social and political modernization also became central to the concept of development. Thus classical political economists like Marx and Ricardo were concerned primarily with economic development, but also addressed concerns about population and broader social issues stemming from industrialization. There were of course different views about the role of Government in driving forward economic growth. For some, it was essential that the Government played a pivotal role. For the neoliberals, it was about allowing market forces to operate without interference, with growth resulting from deregulation, liberalization, and privatization.

Most people would accept that economic growth at a country level and increased material well-being at an individual level are important elements of development. The second does not necessarily follow from the first, however, and even in circumstances where a country's economy is growing rapidly, the better-off tend to benefit disproportionately, and the poor often stay poor. Even just focusing on economic growth as an indicator of developmental progress, therefore, it is important to take into account how the benefits of that growth are distributed across the population.

Most people would also agree that economic growth and disposable income should not be the only key indicators of developmental progress, and that any definition must take 'human development' into account alongside 'economic development'. 'Human development' has been defined in many different ways, but is essentially about giving people the ability to realize the 'potential of human personality'[1] and choices about how to live their lives—the freedom to be able to do certain things, and the freedom not to have to do certain things.[2] Different measures have evolved to try to assess developmental progress, from increases in national and personal income at one end of the scale to efforts to measure happiness and well-being—such as the 'Better life Index' of the Organisation for Economic Cooperation and Development (OECD)—at the other. And the risks of pursuing economic growth without regard to the potential environmental consequences—including but not restricted to climate change—are becoming increasingly evident and are a key indicator in the 'Happy Planet Index' of the New Economics Foundation.

Looking at this from the other end of the telescope, the most common measure of poverty is the $1.25 per capita per day poverty line, now used as the income measure to define 'extreme poverty' (and, as we shall see, the key basis for assessing progress against internationally agreed development targets and goals). But poverty can also be defined in terms of deprivations, and the lack of access to—for example—education and health services, sanitation, and clean drinking water, which can be collated to arrive at a multidimensional poverty index.[3] The aid and development processes designed to help lift people out of poverty can look very different to poor people—sometimes beneficial, occasionally harmful, often simply irrelevant.

It makes sense, then, to consult poor people both as the intended beneficiaries of development and its shapers; in order to be effective, as Collier argues, change must come from within.[4] As we are reminded in the seminal 'Voices of the Poor: Can Anyone Hear Us?', the poor can speak very eloquently for themselves. 'Poor people care about many of the same things that all of us care about: happiness, family, children, livelihood, peace, security, dignity and respect.'[5] Consulting the poor in the process of designing interventions intended to benefit them is likely to lead to better decisions—both by governments and the international community, as argued by Banerjee and Duflo in *Poor Economics*[6] and indeed by business, as argued by Prahalad in *The Fortune at the Bottom of the Pyramid.*[7]

* * *

Those countries which are generally held to be the most 'developed' are those which have in place key elements of physical infrastructure (buildings and transport links) and social and institutional structures that give their citizens the political and economic freedom to make choices about how they live their lives; which provide access to services such as education and health; and which protect their basic human rights. They have generally done this on the basis of many years of political evolution.

'Developing countries' have traditionally been defined as those which have not yet reached any or all of the landmarks noted above including, for example, a strong independent judiciary able to guarantee freedoms and protect the rights of citizens; in which citizens generally continue to rely on agriculture and small-scale farming to subsist; in which there is limited industrial and manufacturing capacity; in which economic growth is at best fitful, and where the benefits are not generally felt by the majority of the population; and where there are significant gaps in the provision of education, health care, and other services.

'Aid' is a word that carries greater baggage; and indeed the whole discourse on aid tends to be characterized by broad and polarized generalizations that reflect strong views and opinions. Much of this is based more on prejudice than research or experience—'aid works' on the one hand, to 'aid is a waste of money' on the other. Even among development 'experts' the range of views is wide and no less polarized.

'Aid' implies a particular sort of relationship—the strong supporting the weak; the rich supporting the poor; the 'haves' supporting the 'have-nots'. That moral argument is crucial, and broadly accepted by most people. But the terms of the debate can easily cross a line into a different sort of discussion, about the competent supporting the incompetent; the well governed supporting the badly governed; smart people giving handouts to their less intelligent and poorer neighbours. As we shall see, this is partly the legacy of the Cold War, when the allocation of aid was driven primarily by political ideology; where corruption was commonplace; and where the notion of 'aid dependency', now rightly seen as a risk and to be avoided, was more likely to be seen as a virtue and to be encouraged.

'Aid' has been generally used to describe the transfer of resources from 'developed' to 'developing' countries (either directly, or via an international organization, or via a non-governmental organization) to support them in the developmental process. It is not, as it is often described, simply a large lump sum of cash passed from a donor to the recipient (some of it, and for a number of donors much of it, including debt relief, scholarships, support for refugees and development awareness, never actually leaves the donor country).

Aid can indeed take the form of a transfer of financial resources ('capital aid'), but can take other forms too—for example, the provision of personnel or advice ('technical assistance' or 'technical cooperation'). It can apply to relatively short-term humanitarian, disaster, or emergency succour or relief on the one hand, or longer-term help and support on the other. It is, particularly in this longer-term context, often referred to as 'official development assistance' (ODA). Where it involves government to government support it is 'bilateral'; where the transfer is from an international body such as the World Bank, it is 'multilateral'. These and other terms are explained at greater length in Part Two.

*　*　*

So far, so (relatively) simple—but ... The division of the world into developed and developing countries; the rich North and the poor South; the haves and the have-nots was always somewhat simplistic, but nevertheless provided a recognizable and reasonable broad historical framework within which to conceptualise aid and development in the second half of the twentieth century. The framework looks rather different in the second decade of the twenty-first century. The world and the relationships between its nations (and indeed between the regions, states, and central authorities comprising those nations) are increasingly complex. Many of the fastest growing economies in the world are now in the 'developing' countries. That is bringing with it prosperity, employment, and opportunities for many (though not for all—and the Arab Spring has shown what can happen when citizens take action in response to a lack of economic opportunity and a closed political system). In the 'developed' countries', economic growth has slowed and for the first time in hundreds of years the younger generation may be less well-off than their parents. The multipolar world of 2015 is a more complicated and nuanced place than the North–South and East–West world of just a few decades before.

Globalization certainly presents opportunities, but it also brings challenges. Many in developing and developed countries alike see it as a threat. In the face of its unknown consequences both states and individuals—particularly those at the margins—respond by seeking to retreat to familiar territory. This is perhaps especially true of the older generation, and is reflected in a wish to turn the clock back to a time when the world was (or seemed to be) more ordered and structured, and their place in it was clearer. This fear of change can result in the growth of religious fundamentalism or, in some countries, at least a push to return to traditional social structures (which may include not allowing girls and women to have access to education, for example). It can also (as is happening in a number of European countries) lead to the growth of extremist political parties whose views tend to encourage the belief that economic, political, and social problems are caused by people and events outside their national borders and their direct control, and that the solution is to close the gates.

Some understanding of these competing pressures is necessary to make sense of what is happening in the world and to make judgements about how to respond politically, economically, and socially. This has both a national and an international dimension. Development and aid are important elements in the mix, and cannot be understood properly without taking into account the broader historical and political context through which they have evolved. The purpose of this book is to show how concepts of aid and development have been shaped by that context and to provide some insights into evolving policy and practice.

* * *

The book is divided into two main parts. The first of these is essentially a narrative, looking at how aid and development thinking have evolved since the end of the Second World War. It describes the context in which a new political and economic order and institutions were developed and shaped for half a century from the mid-1940s, including the process of decolonization and the Cold War. It describes the evolution of International Development Targets (IDTs) and Millennium Development Goals (MDGs), and the North–South dynamics of their implementation. It looks at the key changes since the global financial crisis of 2008, and the breakdown of traditional ideas of 'developed' and 'developing' countries as a number of countries in 'the South' (in particular China and India, but also other countries in Asia and Africa) have made significant progress in the fight against poverty, in large part as a result of their strong economic growth.

It then considers the current debate around a new set of sustainable development goals (SDGs), and the importance of bringing together the three key pillars of economic growth, equity ('leave no-one behind'), and sustainability ('look after the planet'). It suggests that whilst aid will continue to be an important instrument in the battle against poverty, those efforts will concentrate on a decreasing number of individual poor countries and focus increasingly on 'global public goods' (GPGs). It underlines the importance of better-off countries looking not just at their aid performance as an indicator of their commitment to development, but at the full range of policies that impact on less-developed countries. A final chapter takes a look forward over the coming fifteen years, setting out some likely trends in aid and development.

Part Two is designed to complement the narrative account of Part One, and—whilst inevitably being somewhat selective—goes into greater detail about some of the concepts and organizations mentioned there. There are some common definitions (for example, the section on developing country classifications); most disciplines create their own shorthand, language, and acronyms, and the policy and practice of development is no exception. There is more detail on some of the key organizations and institutions (for example, the section on the international financial institutions). And there are some illustrations of how different elements from within and beyond the development community need to combine in a coherent approach to address particular development challenges (for example, the section on security sector reform).

Each of the chapters in Part One has a number of references, as do some of the sections in Part Two. The guiding principles have been that these should not interfere with the narrative flow; they should be light-touch; they should be readily accessible; they should require no detailed technical knowledge to understand; and between them they should provide a balanced range of views on the particular subject under discussion.

Notes

1. Dudley Seers, 'The Meaning of Development'. IDS Communication, 44 (Institute of Development Studies, 1969), pp. 1–26.
2. Amartya Sen, *Development as Freedom* (Oxford: Oxford University Press, 2001).
3. Oxford Poverty and Human Development Initiative, 'Global Multidimensional Poverty Index 2014', <www.ophi.org.uk>.
4. Paul Collier, *The Bottom Billion: Why the Poorest Countries Are Failing and What Can Be Done About It* (New York: Oxford University Press, 2007).
5. Deepa Narayan, *Voices of the Poor: Can Anyone Hear Us?* (New York: Oxford University Press, for the World Bank, 2000).
6. Abhijit V. Banerjee and Esther Duflo, *Poor Economics: A Radical Rethinking of the Way to Fight Global Poverty* (New York: PublicAffairs, 2011).
7. C. K. Prahalad, *The Fortune at the Bottom of the Pyramid: Eradicating Poverty through Profits* (Upper Saddle River, NJ: Prentice Hall, 2005).

PART ONE

1

FROM THE FALL OF
BERLIN TO THE FALL
OF THE BERLIN WALL

The First World War, the 'Great War', fought largely in Europe a century ago, was described as the war to end all wars. Less than a quarter of a century later Europe was again plunged into conflict. The terms of the post-war settlement at Versailles in 1919 in many ways laid the foundations for the subsequent conflict. The League of Nations, set up to provide a framework for conflict resolution and peace-building, proved to be ineffective—in part because increasingly powerful nation-states refused to be directed by an international institution. And the reparations demanded of Germany built up significant resentment which provided fertile ground for Hitler to call for a restoration of national pride through force of arms.

Serious efforts were made to avoid a repetition of these mistakes after the Second World War. There were in that second conflict more military casualties than the first; more civilian deaths (many of them the result of genocide) as a direct result of conflict; and more deaths as a result of war-related famine and disease. It was more of a global conflict, and led to the widespread devastation of towns and infrastructure, particularly (though not exclusively) in Europe. The world could not afford a further repetition, particularly with the invention of the atomic bomb which cast a mushroom-shaped cloud over the future of humankind and threatened its extinction.

So as the tide of battle turned in the direction of the Allied Forces from 1943 onwards, discussions were beginning about the creation of new international bodies which would provide an effective framework for a new political and economic order. It is a testament to those who designed it that, three quarters of a century on, that framework—albeit in need of a major overhaul—broadly remains in place.

On the economic front, those discussions culminated at a Conference at Bretton Woods, New Hampshire in the US in 1944. Those negotiations were about the creation of new institutions to provide oversight of the global economy, and they led to the creation of the International Bank for Reconstruction and Development (IBRD—the World Bank) and the International Monetary Fund (IMF), the so-called 'Bretton Woods institutions' (BWIs).

On the political front, the UN Charter was drawn up at the United Nations Conference in San Francisco. The preamble to the Charter refers to the determination of the peoples of the United Nations 'to promote social progress and better standards of life in larger freedom' and 'to employ international machinery for the promotion of the economic and social advancement of all peoples'. It was complemented by the Universal Declaration of Human Rights in 1948 and its 'recognition of the inherent dignity and of the equal and inalienable rights of all members of the human family' as 'the foundation of freedom, justice and peace in the world'.

Unsurprisingly, the governance structures of these new institutions—how they were to be run—reflected the political and economic realities of the age. There were forty-eight founder members of the UN. The primary decision-making body within the UN was the Security Council, with five permanent members (the 'P5')—the US, the UK, France, Russia, and China, allies in the war effort—and other UN members being elected to the Council on a rotating basis. The Executive Boards of the IMF and IBRD also reflected relative economic power and influence, with single seats for those with the most advanced economies (which included all permanent members of the UN Security Council except China) and other countries grouped into multi-country 'constituencies'.

The primary role of the IBRD was to provide 'soft loans'—financing which, for governments of basically creditworthy countries, was less expensive than borrowing from commercial banks—to support the reconstruction of war-torn Europe, and in particular to rebuild its devastated infrastructure. The IBRD, whose first loan was to France in 1947, initially supported investments in a number of European countries in areas such as dam construction, electricity generation, and the provision of access to water and sanitation.

These loans constituted 'multilateral' support—resources made available by international bodies (in this case at better than market rates, though not sufficiently so as to constitute 'aid' under current definitions). Multilateral organizations by definition represent a broad spectrum of countries and therefore tend to be less politically and ideologically driven than 'bilateral' (or country to country) aid programmes. This does not mean that there were no conditions attached; it is worth noting that in order to qualify for its first IBRD loan France was, at the insistence of the US, required to remove the communist element of its coalition government, reflecting a more assertive shift, from détente to containment, in US foreign policy regarding the Soviet Union. This was defined by the 'Truman Doctrine', under which US President Harry S. Truman pledged to contain communism in Europe and support any country perceived as being threatened by communism or the Soviet Union with both military and economic aid.

The immediate reason for the development of the doctrine was unrest and instability in Greece, and the reduction of involvement by the British, no longer able to provide their traditional support because of their own parlous economic and financial position. Truman believed that there was a strong possibility of Greece falling to communism, with grave consequences for the region, unless it received support. At the same time, it was necessary to support Turkey; whilst Greece and Turkey were rivals, they were both important allies for the Western powers. It was strategically important for them that Turkey should retain control of the Dardanelles passage (Stalin had demanded partial control at the end of the Second World War) between the Black Sea and the Mediterranean.

Thus it was that President Truman appeared before Congress in March 1947 and argued that aid should be given to both Greece and Turkey, not only to help build stability in their relationship but also as part of a broader strategy to provide both military and economic aid to countries whose stability was seen as threatened by communism or the Soviet Union. He requested a total sum of $400 million, noting that a failure to act would not only put at risk peace and stability in and around Greece and Turkey but that the potential domino effect could also compromise the stability of the region as a whole.

Interestingly, President Truman noted that the United Nations might in the normal course of events be expected to take the lead under such circumstances, and referred to the fact that a Commission established by the UN Security Council was investigating alleged border violations. But as far as more substantial support was concerned, 'the situation is an urgent one requiring immediate action and the United Nations and its related organizations are not in a position to extend help of the kind that is required'.[1]

In May 1947, two months after Truman's plea, Congress approved $400 million in economic and military aid (which included advisers, but no military forces) to the region. It was a significant policy development, the first in a series of 'containment' moves by the United States which also included the European Recovery Programme (ERP)—also known as the 'Marshall Plan'—and the creation of the North Atlantic Treaty Organization (NATO) in 1949 (of which both Greece and Turkey became members in 1952). The Truman doctrine effectively guided US foreign policy for over forty years, until the fall of the Berlin Wall signalled the end of the Cold War. From the very beginning, the allocation of aid and economic assistance was linked closely with ideology and the pursuit of broader political objectives.

The ERP was launched in mid-1947 by President Truman's Secretary of State George C. Marshall to support the same broad objectives as IBRD lending, combining very significant sums of aid to support reconstruction and modernization within an agreed framework of cooperation and reconciliation. It was originally conceived, in the immediate aftermath of the Second World War, to include Russia and the Union of Soviet Socialist Republics (USSR). However, Russia was unwilling to subject itself to the scrutiny implicit in the ERP, and—particularly as the relationship with the US deteriorated rapidly in the following years—did not participate (and did not allow any constituent members of the USSR to do so).

On the other hand, it became increasingly evident to the ERP's authors that European recovery would happen only slowly—if at all—unless West Germany became an integral part of the process. Over the four year period of the Plan (1948–52) West Germany benefited increasingly from the ERP's provisions, eventually accounting for some 11 per cent of ERP total expenditure, following the United Kingdom, which was the major recipient (26 per cent) and France (18 per cent). Eighteen European countries in total benefited from the ERP. Some of that support went to the coal and steel industries in countries like Belgium, the Netherlands and Luxembourg, and became a key building block in what was to become the European Coal and Steel Community and then the European Economic Community (EEC). The allocations to Greece and Turkey were over and above the assistance they received under the programme agreed by Congress in response to President Truman's specific request.

The operational provisions of the ERP reflected some of the key aid 'instruments'—mechanisms for getting things done—that still exist (and are defined in greater detail in Part Two). First, there was 'capital aid', which is concessional financial support, often to build or rehabilitate physical infrastructure, or to pay for imported goods. This could take the form of soft loans (financial transfers that needed to be repaid) or grants (financial transfers that didn't need to be repaid). In practice, much of this funding had to be used to pay for (so was 'tied to') manufactured goods and raw materials from the US. Second, there was 'technical assistance'—the transfer of skills rather than money. This took two forms. First, hundreds of technical advisers from the US (and Canada, also effectively undamaged by the conflict) came to Europe to provide advice. Second, hundreds of Europeans went in the other direction to learn direct from industry in North America about new ways of doing business and stimulating growth.

It is often hard to identify the precise effect of aid interventions, as they are almost always part of a larger package of measures involving not only support from a number of members of the international community but also policy change and action by the recipient government. As the history of evolving methods to monitor and evaluate aid interventions demonstrates, it is very difficult to compare 'with' and 'without' cases, and to assess what would have happened to the speed and depth of the European recovery had there been no Marshall Plan. It is, though, worth noting that the period 1948–52—the precise period of the Marshall Plan—was the fastest period of economic growth in European history.

These programmes, and the response from the Eastern bloc, effectively defined the political landscape in Europe for the next forty years. The Soviet Union set up the Council for Mutual Economic Cooperation (COMECON) in January 1949 in response to the creation of the Organisation for European Economic Cooperation (OEEC), which was established in 1948 as a coordinating mechanism for assistance under the Marshall Plan. COMECON comprised mainly the Eastern bloc countries, but also included a number of other countries such as Mongolia, Cuba, and Vietnam sharing a common ideology but at a different stage of economic development—which was also true of a number of countries subsequently admitted as observers, such as Ethiopia, Laos, and South Yemen. In the same way that COMECON was intended to act as a counterbalance to the OEEC, so the Warsaw Pact was established in 1954 in a direct response to the integration of West Germany into NATO.

Whilst the focus of the OEEC initially remained very much on Europe, some of the bodies which would become influential in coordinating and delivering aid and development programmes more widely were established under its auspices. The Overseas Territories

Committee comprising Belgium, France, the Netherlands, Portugal and the United Kingdom was established, for example, to carry out surveys linked to the economic and social development of the overseas territories for which these countries had responsibility. The OEEC in 1961 became the Organisation for Economic Cooperation and Development (OECD), a consortium of the developed countries within but also beyond Europe, including the US and Canada. The inclusion of the word 'development' in the name of the organization reinforced the new dimension of international cooperation and—particularly through the work of its Development Assistance Group (later the Development Assistance Committee)—the increasing importance of relationships with developing countries.

During this period too some of the donor countries set up new bodies to administer their overseas aid. For example, in the UK the Overseas Resources Development Act of 1948 set up the Colonial Development Corporation. In 1957 the European Development Fund (EDF) for Overseas Countries and Territories was set up as part of the Rome treaty which established the EEC. And it comes as no surprise, perhaps, to learn that the US 'Truman Doctrine' led to support not only for the countries of Europe, but more broadly too.

In his inauguration speech of 20 January 1949, President Truman stated the fourth objective of his foreign policy priorities as follows:

> We must embark on a bold new program for making the benefits of our scientific advances and industrial progress available for the improvement and growth of underdeveloped areas. More than half the people of the world are living in conditions approaching misery. Their food is inadequate. They are victims of disease. Their economic life is primitive and stagnant. Their poverty is a handicap and a threat both to them and to more prosperous areas. For the first time in history, humanity possesses the knowledge and skill to relieve the suffering of these people. The United States is pre-eminent among nations in the development of industrial and scientific techniques. The material resources which we can afford to use for assistance of other peoples are limited. But our imponderable resources in technical knowledge are constantly growing and are inexhaustible.[2]

This became known as the 'Point Four Program'—in essence a technical assistance programme for developing countries—and was allocated $25 million for the first year of its operation, fiscal year 1950/1. Whilst it was undoubtedly motivated by a desire to help developing countries move along the development path, it was also linked strongly to the East–West ideological hearts and minds campaign that was beginning to emerge. Truman noted that 'Communist propaganda holds that the free nations are incapable of providing a decent standard of living for the millions of people in under-developed areas of the earth. The Point Four Program will be one of our principal ways of demonstrating the complete falsity of that charge'.[3]

The Act for International Development, which allowed implementation of the Point Four Program, was adopted by Congress in 1950, and the Technical Cooperation Administration (TCA) was established within the Department of State to run it. The Program included within its partner countries Iran, Pakistan, and Israel. Further initiatives under the Truman Administration included the 1952 Mutual Security Act, which provided for major aid programmes for countries including South Korea and Vietnam, administered by the Mutual Security Agency (MSA); the MSA evolved from the Economic Cooperation Agency (ECA) which had administered aid under the Marshall Plan. These programmes were subsequently folded into the Foreign Operations Administration, which ultimately led to the present-day US Agency for International Development, USAID (established under the Foreign Assistance Act of 1961 to administer bilateral economic assistance).

* * *

Something else fed into the mix too. The UN Charter of 1945 established firmly the principle of equal rights and self-determination of peoples. With this, the decolonization process swiftly gathered momentum, beginning in Asia, where the Philippines became independent in 1946, India and Pakistan in 1947, Sri Lanka (then Ceylon) in 1948, and Indonesia in 1950. In Africa, Morocco and Tunisia became independent in 1956 and the process began in sub-Saharan Africa with

Ghana's independence in 1957. Others followed soon after: the East African countries of Kenya, Uganda, and Tanzania (then Tanganyika) in the early 1960s, for example. UN numbers swelled as these countries took up their seats—from 99 in 1960 to 154 by 1980. The process of decolonization continued right until the end of the twentieth century, with Hong Kong reverting from British to Chinese rule in 1997 and Macau from Portuguese to Chinese rule in 1999.

The process was not straightforward, not least because the politics of decolonization became entangled with the politics of the Cold War. The Governments of many of these newly-emerging independent countries professed themselves to be members of the Western or Soviet blocs; those same Governments were often perceived as having been put in place by the former colonial power, and liberation movements were often supported by external governments of the opposite political persuasion. Interestingly, the phrase 'Third World' was originally applied (in 1952) to any country which was not a member of the western ('First World') or the Sino-Soviet ('Second World') blocs; this group evolved into the 'Non-Aligned Movement' in 1961 (and in practice they tended to lean ideologically towards the Soviet bloc). After that, 'Third World' began to be applied to the less well-functioning developing countries.

This all looks like a combustible mix—the major world powers competing for economic, political, and ideological supremacy, and wishing to gain the support of an increasing number of newly independent countries, many of them with significant natural resources but with relatively weak institutions. Nowhere was this mix more combustible than in Africa, though it took some time for that to become evident. The focus in the 1960s was on the erstwhile colonial powers helping to ensure that the constitutional and administrative systems and structures which they had put in place continued to function—desirable both as an end in itself but also as a way of binding those countries into their sphere of influence.

This support came in a number of forms, including of course military cooperation and training. As far as aid was concerned, there were two main forms of support (following the model of the Marshall Plan). First, there was technical assistance, the provision of bureaucratic and professional support, helping to build local capacity until the country became self-sustaining. Much of this comprised expatriates living and working in those countries, though there was also a significant element of training by bringing students and professionals to hone their skills in universities and colleges in Europe and elsewhere, often of course with the former colonial power.

Along with the provision of expertise came the provision of financial support, or 'capital aid'. This was generally in the form of grants, at that time mainly for the support of specific projects—the construction and maintenance of hospitals and schools, for example, or of road and rail infrastructure. This was largely 'tied' to procurement of project-related expenditure in the country providing the assistance.

The beneficiaries of this support were on the whole the better-off members of society, the governing classes who had largely inherited (or seized) power from the former colonial powers. The behaviour of those governing classes—their respect for human rights, for example, or the extent to which they sought to introduce more democratic systems of government—mattered considerably less as a criterion for support than did their ideological leanings: aid was part of the mix which sought to ensure that they remained on the right side of the ideological divide.

This is not to say that aid was generally ineffective or used for the wrong purposes: it supported many crucial interventions, both technical and financial. The literature of aid and development is filled with evidence from supporters and detractors of its efficacy or failures. The truth is that aid can be extremely effective under some circumstances and completely ineffective (or positively counterproductive) in others. Few people, though, would argue about the success of the 'Green Revolution' in Asia in the 1960s and 1970s—a process supported by scientific and technical expertise from the international community—which transformed agricultural productivity in India and other countries in South Asia and not only helped prevent mass starvation but provided the basis for development in other areas (this is described in greater detail in the section on 'Food Security and Food Aid' in Part Two).

What exactly was this 'aid' anyway? Attempts were being made to ensure that there were clearer definitions of what could and what could not be counted as 'aid', largely within the Development Assistance Committee of the OECD. This set up mechanisms to monitor the performance of individual donor countries, for example, and agreed definitions of what could and could not be counted as 'official development assistance' (ODA). It was concerned both about the quantity of aid—the volume of concessional resources being made available—and also quality; the impact and effectiveness which aid programmes had on the countries in which they were operating, and on the people who were the ultimate beneficiaries.

In 1970, many of the OECD countries (though excluding some like the US) agreed a commitment to devote 0.7 per cent of their 'gross national product' (GNP)—their wealth—to ODA. This did not seem like a massive commitment, on the face of it—though in practice only a small number of countries, largely in Scandinavia, have ever reached that target. In 2013, the United Kingdom became the first of the 'G7' countries—the largest OECD economies—to do so. That is, though, to jump ahead a very long way...

* * *

For many developing countries, these concessional financial flows mattered a great deal, constituting the bulk of their external resources and a significant proportion of their budgets. This of course gave the donor community tremendous leverage over those countries' economic policies which—combined with what they saw as the inequitable balance of power within the major global political and economic institutions—was resented and resisted by a number of them, who worked hard in support of the creation of a 'New International Economic Order' (NIEO). This had its origins in the early 1960s, when the UN General Assembly agreed to a one-off meeting in Geneva in 1964 to discuss a range of trade, investment, and economic development issues. Out of this was born the United Nations Conference on Trade and Development (UNCTAD), which became a permanent UN institution (based in Geneva), primarily used as a forum for developing countries to advocate measures which would allow them to have greater participation in (and secure greater benefits from) the global economy.

For some members of UNCTAD, that meant not just measures to ensure fairer commodity prices or to protect the interests of particularly vulnerable states, but a root and branch review of the international system, from which they felt excluded. There was a major debate at the UNCTAD meeting of 1972 in Santiago on the issue of voting rights (and the allocation of Special Drawing Rights, or SDRs, in the IMF), which split those developing countries determined to press for fundamental change from the milder (mainly Latin American) advocates of reform. This led to a weakening of their overall negotiating position, and there was no agreement at that stage beyond an understanding that the issues would be considered further. The high point of the campaign came in May 1974 with a Resolution[4] adopted in the UN General Assembly in support of the establishment of an NIEO, on the back of significant shocks to the global economic system, not least the oil crisis of 1973–4 and others in 'a series of grave crises which have had severe repercussions, especially on the developing countries because of their generally greater vulnerability to external economic impulses'.

The Resolution does not mince its words, referring to the continuation of 'vestiges of alien and colonial domination, foreign occupation, racial discrimination, apartheid and neo-colonialism', asserting that 'it has proved impossible to achieve an even and balanced development of the international community under the existing international economic order', and recommending a revised system which involves 'the active, full and equal participation of the developing countries in the formulation and application of all decisions that concern the international community'. In truth, the very power imbalances which the NIEO was intended to address meant that there was little progress then—and has been little since—on these issues, though as we will see the logic for reform of the global economic and political order has become increasingly compelling.

* * *

With the 0.7 per cent target in place, questions were raised about the purpose and targets of ODA, and whether it represented good value for money. Much of this debate took place within the Development Assistance Committee of the OECD, which took on an increasingly important role in monitoring the quality and quantity of donor financial flows and in ensuring that aid was targeted at poverty reduction. Attempts were made by a number of people in key positions—such as the British Minister for Overseas Development, Judith Hart, who in 1975 produced a White Paper entitled 'More Help for the Poorest', and Robert McNamara, then President of the World Bank, former US defence secretary and deeply influenced by his experience of the Vietnam War—to push development policy increasingly towards helping the poorest people in the poorest countries. But in practice a key and continuing driver of aid policy and priorities was its value as a tool to support ideological allies.

There was nothing secret about this; it was completely explicit as a policy objective of governments in both East and West. In the UK, the government of Margaret Thatcher which took office in May 1979 integrated the Ministry of Overseas Development into the Foreign Office; issued a policy document in 1980 stating clearly that aid would increasingly be used to support political and commercial objectives; and created packages of aid and export credit funding to underwrite the activities of British businesses in the developing world. Mrs Thatcher was heavily influenced by Peter Bauer's critique of aid.[5] In the US, her ideological soulmate Ronald Reagan spoke strongly in favour of 'the magic of the marketplace'; and US development assistance remained closely tied to ensuring that aid resources benefited US companies as much as possible.

Again, this is not to say that many aid projects did not achieve very positive results, or that many aid practitioners did not try very hard to ensure that they brought about real benefits to aid recipients. But because the allocation of resources was determined to a large degree by political considerations, and because the beneficiaries were often government elites, there was some truth in the adage that aid represented the transfer of resources from the poor in rich countries to the rich in poor countries (and yes, some aid funds undoubtedly ended up in the personal Swiss bank accounts of corrupt and unsavoury leaders). It was not an easy environment within which to focus on developmental objectives and the reduction of poverty. Within the donor countries, opinions about the role and effectiveness of aid polarized—in no area more clearly than structural adjustment, which also caused consternation in some developing countries, where the IMF and World Bank insisted on a number of fundamental and politically controversial reforms in exchange for their support.

Many developing countries faced an immediate and major fiscal adjustment problem in the wake of the 1979 energy crisis. There were two possible responses to this. One was to restructure budgets so as to reduce the deficit; the other was keep spending, which sowed the seeds of rapid inflation, undermining growth and impoverishing the worst off. Tough structural reform measures were under way in the UK and the US, and the need for such measures and a strong focus on market forces were reflected increasingly in IMF and World Bank policies, and specifically their emphasis on 'structural adjustment'. Potential borrowers were basically required to reduce inflation and their fiscal imbalance, which often led to a reduction in social spending and rises in the price of food (as subsidies were reduced). This combination of measures was subsequently referred to as the 'Washington consensus'—though it was in practice never quite clear whether there was such a consensus or, if there was. exactly what that entailed.

Structural adjustment programmes (SAPs) got a bad press. There is no doubt that they impacted heavily on the poorest people, and in a scathing criticism in the late 1980s UNICEF reported that SAPs had been responsible for 'reduced health, nutritional, and educational levels for tens of millions of children in Asia, Latin America, and Africa'.[6] The reality was somewhat more nuanced. In practice many public expenditures, especially subsidies, were of greatest benefit to the better off in developing countries, and it was not entirely coincidental that it was developing country governments dominated by elites who protested most vigorously about the alleged injustice of structural adjustment.

Structural adjustment was not—or should not have been—just about an exclusive focus on public finances and fiscal imbalances, but about other policy areas where there were obstacles to development, and how to stimulate growth and protect poor people. So in Morocco, for example, the abolition of the export monopoly on fruits, vegetables, and preserved fish (which primarily benefited the elite) led to a massive jump in income for poor producers. In Uganda, the abolition of the Coffee Marketing Board, which was again diverting very large sums into the pockets of the elite, led to an increase in the share of the producer price from 25 to 65 per cent of the world price.

* * *

On the economic front, the 1980s were generally a decade best forgotten. On the political front, meanwhile, what was a Cold War in Europe was becoming an increasingly hot war in many parts of the developing world, and particularly in Africa. Opposition movements, in many cases purporting to be of a different ideological persuasion from the governments to which they were opposed, were often supported politically and financially by members of the international community of the same ideological persuasion; so conflict often became in effect proxy wars between the West and East.

Members of the international community were also keen to ensure continuing access to the natural resources which were abundant in Africa, following 'the scramble for Africa'[7] which had characterized European interventions in the continent in the second half of the nineteenth century and which are described in detail in Thomas Pakenham's excellent book of that name. One hundred and fifty years ago much of Africa remained unknown and unexplored by Europeans. Of course, there was a long history of trade with Africa north of the Sahara. Parts of West Africa (the focus of the slave trade to the Caribbean and North America) were also well-known. But little was known about much of Africa's interior until explorers such as Richard Burton, John Speke, and David Livingstone embarked on various expeditions. They encountered Arab slave-traders on their journeys, and subsequently Livingstone, the well-known explorer-missionary who died in 1873, called for action to combat the slave trade in East Africa by opening up the continent through the three Cs—Commerce, Christianity and Civilization.

Just a dozen years after Livingstone's death the General Act of Berlin was signed on 26 February 1885. It was a major step in dividing Africa among the European states. In spite of language about the moral and physical benefits to the native population as a result of the civilizing influence of the Europeans—the second and third of Livingstone's three 'Cs'—in practice the Berlin Treaty was almost overwhelmingly a reflection of the first 'C' and reflected the commercial ambitions of the European countries, a political settlement negotiated between them and designed to achieve their (often competing) strategic and economic objectives.

Under the Treaty, the interior of Africa was to be freely accessible to all, and the Congo basin a free trade area under what at the time was (mistakenly) perceived to be the philanthropic oversight of King Leopold of the Belgians. By the beginning of the twentieth century 90 per cent of Africa was under European control.

* * *

In the early 1960s, as countries around the world gained their independence, it was assumed that the countries of Africa, with their significant natural resources, would take off and the countries of eastern and southern Asia, less well endowed, would be left behind. The term 'basket case' was applied in 1971 by then US Secretary of State Henry Kissinger to the nascent Bangladesh. But even then the so-called 'Green Revolution' of the 1960s, which in particular created stronger, drought-resistant varieties of rice, was helping to ensure that large-scale famine in Asia was becoming a thing of the past. Many Asian countries started to make significant developmental progress long before the end of the Cold War, and 'basket cases' became a term increasingly associated with Africa. Development has no greater enemies than conflict and insecurity; nowhere demonstrates that better than Africa.

And no country demonstrates that better within Africa than Ethiopia in the 1980s. Colonel Mengistu led a coup which overthrew Emperor Haile Selassie in 1974, and an increasingly bloody crackdown in the mid-1970s led to the creation of a strengthening resistance movement in the north of the country. The combination of conflict and harvest failure in the north led to the famine of 1984, in which over a million people out of a population of 30 million people died. There was in truth no shortage of food in the country as a whole; but Mengistu used the opportunity to punish the rebels and the rural communities who were supporting them by withholding supplies.

Children with staring, blank eyes, matchstick limbs, and distended bellies remain for many people the archetypal image of Ethiopia and Africa. But perception can take decades to catch up with reality; thirty years on, Ethiopia has one of the fastest growing economies in the world, and its development has been extraordinary—and its success is by no means unique in Africa, or indeed in the developing world as a whole. Terms like 'developing world' now seem increasingly old-fashioned, or at least partial, not reflecting the more complex world of the first half of the twenty-first century rather than the North–South, East–West certainties of the second half of the twentieth century. And it is precisely because of the end of the East–West divide that the end of the North–South divide has become possible.

2

A DECADE OF CHANGE
IN THE 1990s

A New Focus on Poverty and Governance

It is hard to overemphasize the significance of the fall of the Berlin Wall at the end of 1989. It was the end result of years of political adjustment, particularly within the Union of Soviet Socialist Republics (USSR). Put simply, it was becoming increasingly evident that the Soviet system was not working, either politically or economically. The options were for the ruling parties across eastern and central Europe, and in Russia in particular, to provide more of the political and economic freedoms for which their people were asking, or to risk growing internal dissent which could bring about those changes in a more violent and revolutionary way.

Much of the credit for the way in which change happened goes to President Gorbachev of Russia, and in turn the constructive relationships which he formed with Presidents Reagan and Bush senior in Washington. 'Perestroika' ('restructuring') and 'glasnost' ('openness') became part of the English-speaking lexicon. It was touch and go whether the East German military would fire on their citizens and those of West Germany as they reached out to each other through the wall. They did not.

This contrasts, incidentally, with events in Beijing earlier the same year, where student protests had taken place in Tiananmen Square at the same time as the annual meetings of the Asian Development Bank (ADB), at which many donor representatives were also present. It seemed for a few days as if a similar thaw was taking place within

China, with a willingness to loosen the iron grip of the Communist Party. But while there were certainly members of the Politburo who wished to move in this direction, the protests were brutally put down after the delegates to the ADB meeting had packed their bags and left. Opening up would come—but not yet.

Back in Europe, the change process moved ahead inexorably, if not yet inevitably. In Russia itself, the influence of the Communist Party waned only gradually, and there was strong resistance to change in some quarters, including parts of the military machine, leading to protests and counterprotests and marches on the streets of Moscow, with the risk of reversion to the old order only narrowly averted. In other parts of the former USSR, where any tradition of market-based institutions was weaker and buried in a more distant past, and where reform was seen as an insult added to the injury of a loss of empire and global standing, the ruling elites struggled to cling on to power and to resist the economic and political shifts which had the potential to suck away their power base.

Elsewhere in eastern and central Europe, the changes happened swiftly and with the overwhelming support of the population in countries like the Baltic States (Latvia, Lithuania, and Estonia), Poland, Hungary, and Czechoslovakia. The far-reaching institutional and economic reforms that were necessary, but initially painful, were welcomed in those countries, which had a long tradition of liberal government interrupted for only a relatively brief period of Soviet domination—from which those reforms represented liberation. They included political reforms such as the introduction of (or in some cases return to) parliamentary democracy; respect for human rights, including through putting in place a strong and independent judiciary; and economic reforms such as reducing the role of state-owned enterprises and opening up the market to competition.

There was international political and economic support for these changes, albeit not on the scale of the Marshall Plan. New schemes were set up by existing donors such as the UK (the 'Know-How Funds') and EU (the TACIS and PHARE programmes) to provide technical support for reform programmes, and a major new bank—the European Bank for Reconstruction and Development (EBRD)—was created to provide financial support for projects and programmes within the countries of eastern and central Europe. There was, too, a powerful external incentive to change, in the form of potential membership of the European Community. This would bring with it access to regional development grants and structural funds, and support regional economic integration.

* * *

Of course the implications of these momentous changes reverberated around the world, not least in developing countries. The ending of the East–West ideological split had profound consequences for the countries of the South and the North–South relationship too. First, those governments or resistance movements which were closely aligned with Marxist or communist philosophy suddenly found themselves without state sponsors. Second, it opened up political space for the donor community to ask themselves serious questions about the justification for their aid and development programmes, now that one of the key pillars of that justification—the need to provide economic and political support to certain countries, no matter how corrupt or dysfunctional, to keep them on the right side of the political divide—was no longer relevant.

The requirements asked of the countries of central and eastern Europe for aid support, and in preparation for potential membership of the European Union, provided a model for the realignment of overseas aid policies in the early 1990s. Recipient governments needed to set out clear policies of political and economic reform, embracing principles of human rights and parliamentary democracy and opening up their economies to the private sector. And they had to demonstrate that their policies broadly benefited all the people of their country and not just the governing elites.

One of the regrettable consequences of aid policies during the Cold War period, given the strong focus on the political and commercial benefits to the donor country, was that significant resources were often provided to governments with appalling records on—for example—human rights and transparency. So aid programmes and projects could actually disadvantage vulnerable and minority groups in-country, and it was not always possible to put in place the checks and balances required to ensure that aid funds were used as intended and did not end up in the private overseas bank accounts of government leaders or members of their families.

The nature and composition of aid programmes changed significantly during the early 1990s. Bilateral donors tended to move away from support for major infrastructure projects and the natural resources sectors, leaving these increasingly to the major multilateral donors (the World Bank, the regional development banks and the European Commission), and focused instead on the promotion of economic and political reform, greater transparency, and social inclusion. This was on the whole less capital-intensive, and total ODA actually declined for seven successive years following the end of the Cold War.

As the programmes changed, so did the nature of those who administered them. Engineers and agricultural specialists made way for governance and social development advisers, who looked for example to strengthen legal and judicial systems and to ensure that the rights of under-represented and marginalized groups were safeguarded in the process of development. The donor community was powerful, and because they still contributed a very significant proportion of the budget in many developing countries were able to insist on many of these changes.

The World Bank traditionally chaired meetings of the 'Consultative Group' (CG) for those countries, which met (usually once a year) at the Bank's office in Paris, providing donors with an opportunity to quiz the ministers responsible for finance and economic development about their policies and to indicate the possible levels of their continuing support. While in earlier years CG meetings were largely pro forma affairs, where difficult issues were not publically aired, this began to change in the early 1990s, when donors became more assertive about stating conditions—often relating to better governance—for their continued support. At a CG meeting for Kenya, for example, donors took the unprecedented step of declining to make new aid pledges until the government had taken action to address serious corruption issues.

In parallel with these developments, a new instrument aimed at strengthening commitment to reform and coordination of donor efforts around a specific set of policy goals was developed—the so-called Policy Framework Paper (PFP). In theory, the PFP was supposed to be a recipient-government document, but in practice it was prepared by IMF staff (and, in some cases, by joint Bank–IMF staff teams). Since the existence of an agreed PFP was a requirement of IMF support and budget support from the Bank, there was significant pressure to ensure that one was prepared, even in the face of limited government commitment.

By the late 1990s, the power dynamic had shifted significantly. Consultative Group meetings were chaired by finance ministers of the country concerned, rather than by senior World Bank officials, and held increasingly in-country. Whilst this probably weakened donors' ability to influence outcomes and ensure that their funds were properly used (particularly in countries where government's interest in achieving broad-based development was less than whole-hearted), it nevertheless reflected the properly central role of progressive governments in the management and coordination of aid, and in that sense was a very positive development.

At the same time, policy as well as implementation responsibility for donor programmes shifted increasingly from capitals to the field. As a result of growing peace and stability, economies began to strengthen and become less reliant on external support—so the relative influence of the donor community over policy decisions gradually lessened. And a new generation of leaders in Africa and elsewhere became increasingly influential, determined to carve out the developmental path for their countries rather than have it carved out for them by the international community.

Nevertheless, the role of the international community remained strong, and by the mid-1990s discussions were beginning in the Development Assistance Committee of the OECD and elsewhere about how to capture some of the positive shifts in development policy—and in particular the need for development to be inclusive and to address the challenges faced by the poorest people in the poorest countries. It is to that discussion that we now turn.

* * *

Was it possible to conceive of a world not only in which the lot of the poorest people in the poorest countries could be improved, but in which poverty itself could be eliminated? In the mid-1990s nearly a quarter of the world's population lived in absolute poverty, defined then as living on less than $1 per head per day. And nearly three-quarters of those were women and girls, with no access to health services or schools.

Government aid agencies, international and non-governmental organizations (NGOs) had long talked of doing themselves out of a job in the long term, but was there now a possibility of taking steps towards this objective? It would have seemed madness to believe so in the mid-1980s, the darkest hours of the Cold War before the dawn symbolized by the tearing down of the Berlin Wall, but it did not seem to be quite such a stretch a decade on.

The two reports of the Brandt Commission in 1979 (North–South: A Programme for Survival)[1] and 1983 (Common Crisis)[2] stressed the importance of making progress on development issues, but were rather downbeat in their assessment; the second report, tellingly, was more pessimistic than the first. Many of their themes were picked up in the Brundtland report (Our Common Interest)[3] of 1987, which focused in particular on the threats to the environment, including the emergence of holes in the ozone layer allowing harmful rays to pass into the atmosphere. And it noted the impact of a rapidly increasing world population, which stood at 2.3 billion people in 1945 and had doubled by the time the report was published (it is now more than three times that number, and continues to grow).

In the Foreword to *Our Common Interest*, Mrs Brundtland recognized the importance of dealing with international development and environmental (or 'sustainable development') issues together. She says:

> The environment does not exist as a sphere separate from human actions, ambitions, and needs, and attempts to defend it in isolation from human concerns have given the very word 'environment' a connotation of naivety in some political circles. The word 'development' has also been narrowed by some into a very limited focus, along the lines of 'what poor nations should do to become richer', and thus again is automatically dismissed by many in the international arena as being a concern of specialists, of those involved in questions of 'development assistance'.

But—she continues—the 'environment is where we all live; and "development" is what we all do in attempting to improve our lot within that abode. The two are inseparable'.

Mrs Bruntland's observations are acute and to the point. They were reinforced powerfully by cosmologist and philosopher Carl Sagan, who was present at the launch of the *Voyager* 1 spacecraft in August 1977, and again in February 1990—just a few weeks after the fall of the Berlin Wall—as it sped towards the edge of the solar system, its cameras pointing forward into uncharted space. Sagan instructed that the cameras be reversed. They picked up, just visible against the vastness of space, what Sagan describes as 'a pale blue dot', on which everyone who had ever lived, every king and queen, every pauper and peasant, had been born and had died, on which every act of war and peace, of cruelty and compassion, had been played out. Sagan comes to the end of his description thus:

> There is perhaps no better demonstration of the folly of human conceits than this distant image of our tiny world. To me, it underscores our responsibility to deal more kindly with one another and to preserve and cherish the pale blue dot, the only home we've ever known.[4]

These comments from Brundtland and Sagan help frame a number of the issues exercising the international community a quarter of a century later. In the shorter term, many of the key themes emerging from the Brundtland report were picked up at the Rio de Janeiro 'Earth Summit' in 1992, which led to some important formal outcomes such as the creation of the UN Framework Convention on Climate Change; the Convention on Biological Diversity; and the Convention to Combat Desertification.

The Rio summit was but one of a number of international conferences in the early 1990s on a range of issues which provided key themes and objectives for those looking to develop a set of objectives and aspirations for international development. For example, the Jomtien World Conference on 'Education for All' in 1990 talks about universal access to education, including women and girls. The Conference on Population and Development in Cairo in 1994 referred to the importance of enabling people to have choices about the number and timing of their children, and of reducing maternal mortality. The World Food Summit in 1996 set a target of reducing the number of undernourished people in the world by half.

So for those setting out to build a set of global objectives for international development assistance, there were a number of international agreements—or at least aspirations—already in place which could form the basic framework. And that is exactly what happened in the creation of the 'International Development Targets'.

*   *   *

The intention of the International Development Targets (IDTs; see Box 1)—also referred to as the International Development Goals— was to provide a number of milestones against which progress towards poverty elimination could be measured. Building on earlier conferences and international agreements, they comprised three key elements around economic well-being, human development, and environmental sustainability and regeneration.

The IDTs had their origins in discussions within the Development Assistance Committee (DAC) of the OECD, and specifically in a document produced for the DAC High Level Meeting in May 1996 called: 'Shaping the Twenty-First Century: The Contribution of Development Cooperation'. In addition to their intrinsic merit, the IDTs

---

BOX 1 The International Development Targets

Economic Well-being
- A reduction by one-half in the proportion of people living in extreme poverty by 2015

Human Development
- universal primary education in all countries by 2015
- demonstrated progress towards gender equality and the empowerment of women by eliminating gender disparity in primary and secondary education by 2005
- a reduction by two-thirds in the mortality rates for infants and children under age 5 and a reduction by three-fourths in maternal mortality, all by 2015
- access through the primary health-care system to reproductive health services for all individuals of appropriate ages as soon as possible and no later than the year 2015

Environmental Sustainability and Regeneration
- the implementation of national strategies for sustainable development in all countries by 2005, so as to ensure that current trends in the loss of environmental resources are effectively reversed at both global and national levels by 2015

---

gained traction because they attracted strong political support in a number of the donor countries. In the UK, the incoming Labour Government in 1997 used the IDTs as the focus of a White Paper called *Eliminating World Poverty: A Challenge for the 21st Century*. Under the leadership of Clare Short, the newly created Department for International Development aspired to global leadership on international development issues. The UK committed to focus on the achievement of the IDTs; to ensure that all its future support was in the form of grants rather than loans; and to abolish the tying of UK aid to the provision of UK goods and services. The Secretary of State found powerful allies in her Norwegian, Dutch, and German counterparts—as it happens, all of them women—who between them comprised the informal but influential 'Utstein Group' (named after one of their meetings at Utstein Abbey in Western Norway).

The new President of the World Bank, James Wolfensohn, also believed that the Bank had to make poverty reduction more central to lending decisions. He was a strong advocate of borrowing countries putting together a 'Comprehensive Development Framework' (CDF), which would set out clearly how countries intended to address a whole range of issues that were holding back poverty reduction in their countries. He was of course right that poverty reduction requires a comprehensive approach, but there was nervousness among some shareholders that this would provide a justification for expanding the already overstretched mandate of the Bank, and would lead the Bank into becoming involved in political issues (which its Articles precluded). Many of the ideas in the CDF were thus folded into what became a key document for both the IMF and World Bank (and other members of the international community), the Poverty Reduction Strategy Paper (PRSP).

In the early 1990s, there was a growing recognition in the IMF (under its Managing Director Michel Camdessus, later to become a member of the Commission for Africa) and World Bank that many countries, especially Low Income Countries (LICs) in Africa, faced unsustainable debt burdens, which were greatly hampering their ability to tackle poverty. Much of that debt had been incurred to pay for arms imports; the Cold War cast a long shadow. This led to the launch of the Highly Indebted Poor Countries (HIPC) initiative in 1996, with the aim of ensuring that no poor country faced a debt burden which it was unable to manage.

In due course, the production of a PRSP became a condition for countries to be considered for HIPC support. Countries also had to be eligible to borrow from the World Bank's concessional lending agency, the International Development Association, and from the IMF's Poverty Reduction and Growth Trust; to face an unsustainable debt burden that could not be addressed through traditional debt relief mechanisms; and to have established a sound track record of reform and the implementation of sound policies.

PRSPs were launched in 1999 as successors to the PFPs, and were designed to promote a comprehensive country-based and country-owned strategy for poverty reduction—part of that same shift aimed at much stronger country ownership of the Consultative Group process, a shift which also led to the increasing centrality of the International Development Targets and their key objective of a substantial reduction in the proportion of people living in absolute poverty.

PRSPs were intended to be based on five core principles. They should be:

> country-driven, promoting national ownership of strategies through broad-based participation of civil society;
>
> result-oriented, and focused on outcomes that would benefit the poor;
>
> comprehensive, in recognizing the multidimensional nature of poverty;
>
> partnership-oriented, involving the coordinated participation of development partners (government, domestic stakeholders, and external donors); and
>
> based on a long-term perspective for poverty reduction.

There has been some criticism that the PRSPs (like their predecessors, the PFPs) have been driven (and much of them drafted) by the staff of the BWIs, and that there has been in some cases scant evidence of the participatory process (particularly with domestic stakeholders and civil society) which is one of the PRSP requirements. There was certainly some force in those criticisms in the early years of the PRSP, though in a number of cases this was about capacity within the developing countries rather than a lack of willingness to own and deliver them. There is equally no doubt that they have become increasingly country-owned over time and are now key documents both for the countries concerned and for the international donor community—not least as indicators of the seriousness with which countries approached the need to make progress towards the International Development Targets or, more accurately, towards what the IDTs were to become.

3

NEW DEVELOPMENT TARGETS FOR A NEW MILLENNIUM

The MDGs

The Millennium Declaration[1], agreed at the UN General Assembly meetings in September 2000, is by any standards an extraordinary document. Every nation in the world signed up to it, and committed themselves to promoting democracy and the rule of law, as well as respect for all internationally recognized human rights and fundamental freedoms, including the right to development and to work collectively for more inclusive political processes, allowing genuine participation by all citizens in all their countries. The Declaration has a section specifically on the need for special measures to address the particular challenges of poverty eradication and sustainable development in Africa.

The Declaration refers to the responsibility of UN member states *to uphold the principles of human dignity, equality and equity at the global level.* It refers to the responsibility of world leaders and their duty *to all the world's peoples, especially the most vulnerable and in particular, the children of the world, to whom the future belongs.* It says that *Men and Women have the right to live their lives and raise their children in dignity, free from hunger and from the fear of violence, oppression or injustice.* It commits member states to sparing *no effort to free our fellow men, women and children from the abject and dehumanizing conditions of extreme poverty and to freeing the entire human race from want.* The Declaration goes on to recognize the importance of environmental protection, and in particular sparing future generations *the threat of living on a planet irredeemably spoilt by human activities* and reaffirms its support for the principles of sustainable development and *a new ethic of conservation and stewardship.*

The Millennium Declaration is a powerful statement of intent, in particular recognizing the importance of a conducive enabling political environment within which development can take place. There is in general, though, a lack of specificity and mechanisms by which to monitor the implementation of its provisions on issues like rights and democracy. Some might say that this lack of time-bound and monitorable objectives encouraged some countries which had no serious intention of following through on those commitments to sign up—a type of expediency which would not be unprecedented in international diplomacy.

There is one exception to this general lack of quantifiable objectives: paragraph 19 (see Box 2) picks up and develops some of the key elements of the International Development Targets, notably the commitment to halve by 2015 the proportion of people living in absolute poverty.

Paragraph 19 of the Declaration, in addition to the overarching poverty reduction objective, thus included targets very similar to the IDTs on primary education, maternal mortality, and child health; omitting those on access to reproductive health services and the environment; and adding new ones on HIV/AIDS and improving the lives of slum-dwellers. This went some way towards providing the specificity required for developing countries to use the Declaration (and for the donor countries to do likewise) as a planning tool for achieving specific outcomes by specific dates. There was, however, some potential to strengthen the links to the IDTs, and similarly to strengthen the links to goals which had been previously set within the UN system and which could be both implemented and tracked.

Setting goals was not a new departure for the UN. They have indeed been an integral part of its operation, with extensive debate and discussion on a particular theme often culminating in a conference

---

BOX 2 Para 19, United Nations Millennium Declaration

We resolve further:

- To halve, by the year 2015, the proportion of the world's people whose income is less than one dollar a day and the proportion of people who suffer from hunger and, by the same date, to halve the proportion of people who are unable to reach or to afford safe drinking water.
- To ensure that, by the same date, children everywhere, boys and girls alike, will be able to complete a full course of primary schooling and that girls and boys will have equal access to all levels of education.
- By the same date, to have reduced maternal mortality by three quarters, and under-five mortality by two thirds, of their current rates.
- To have, by then, halted and begun to reverse, the spread of HIV/AIDS, the scourge of malaria and other diseases that afflict humanity.
- To provide special assistance to children orphaned by HIV/AIDS.
- By 2020, to have achieved a significant improvement in the lives of at least 100 million slum dwellers as proposed in the 'Cities Without Slums' initiative.

---

with a communique setting out what has been agreed, and by when results should be delivered. The Jomtien conference on education and the Cairo conference on population in the 1990s have already been noted; in fact the first education conferences were organized by UNESCO around 1960, and set goals for the expansion of primary to tertiary education. The UN General Assembly set goals for economic growth for the 1960s as part of the 'Development Decade'; developing countries were to attain an overall growth rate of 5 per cent (in fact they did slightly better than that), and the developed countries were to transfer public capital flows of 1 per cent of GNP, including aid (in fact they did slightly worse). This set the scene for the

1970s, the second Development Decade, and the establishment of the 0.7 per cent ODA:GNP target already noted.

Other goals have covered a range of issues, many relating to education, health, and the environment. The prime responsibility for achieving the goals has quite properly rested with the governments of the countries they were intended to benefit, with explicit or implicit support through increases in ODA from the international donor community. In practice, experience demonstrated that the sharper the focus of the goal, the greater the likelihood of success. In 1966, the UN set itself the target of eradicating smallpox within 10 years, an objective it achieved just one year late when it identified the last case of smallpox in Somalia in 1977. Efforts towards the eradication of guinea worm and polio have also been extremely successful.

So the architects of a new set of goals had to seek to achieve a very difficult balance. Any new goals had to be comprehensive and ambitious. They had to build on the Millennium Declaration and the International Development Targets. They had to be simple, with a sharp focus, but reflect a very complex reality. They also had to recognize the politics of the situation: once specific targets and measurable indicators on rights, democratization, human dignity, equity, and access to family planning services became part of the equation, the terrain immediately became more difficult.

They had to have support from developing countries, on whom the main burden for putting in place the policy changes to deliver any goals would fall, and from the donor community (who would need to make commitments to support those changes). And it was important to bring alongside these efforts the other key players in the international community; as well as the OECD's Development Assistance Committee (DAC), the International Monetary Fund (IMF) and World Bank needed to be brought on board, inevitably with a perspective focused on economic growth and service provision as the key to poverty reduction rather than on rights and equity. There was an implicit Compact, which was 'to encourage sustainable pro-poor development progress and donor support of domestic efforts in this direction'.[2]

A series of consultations took place between the UN and other members of the international community such as the World Bank and the DAC. In September 2001—in response to a request from the UN General Assembly at the end of the previous year, and as an Annex to the first Millennium Summit follow-up Report *We the Peoples: The Role of the United Nations in the 21st Century*—Kofi Annan was able to launch the 'Road Map for the Implementation of the Millennium Development Goals' (MDGs—see Box 3).

It is probably true to say that the enthusiasm for implementing most international understandings and agreements fades over time. The MDGs have if anything gained in political resonance, and have been used increasingly by developing countries and donors in their policy and planning processes. They are now readily referred to by developing countries reluctant to embrace them in their early years because they were seen as largely donor-driven. Those countries include China (in particular) and India, where hundreds of millions of people have emerged from poverty, and they have also become a touchstone for the activities of donor agencies, even in those countries which were initially reluctant to accept them. Those countries included the US, but they have been used by USAID increasingly as the focus of their development efforts.

All this is in spite of the fact that the Annex to the Secretary-General's 'Road Map' was never formally endorsed by the UN membership, but was merely described as 'a useful guide' in the relevant UN General Assembly resolution. The MDGs continue to be a touchstone for the significant successes as well as the occasional failures of international development over the past decade and a half. They have the benefit of being memorable, achieved in large part by creating a limited number of goals (eight), identifying a number of more detailed targets linked to specific goals, and coming up with a series of indicators which would show whether or not progress was happening.

BOX 3 The Millennium Development Goals

Goal 1. Eradicate extreme poverty and hunger
• Halve the proportion of people living in absolute poverty by 2015
• Halve the proportion of people who suffer from hunger by 2015

Goal 2. Achieve universal primary education
• Ensure that by 2015 children everywhere, boys and girls alike, will
  be able to complete a full course of primary schooling

Goal 3. Promote gender equality and empower women
• Eliminate gender disparity in primary and secondary education,
  preferably by 2005, and in all levels of education no later than
  2015

Goal 4. Reduce child mortality
• Reduce by two-thirds the under-five mortality rate by 2015

Goal 5. Improve maternal health
• Reduce by three-quarters the maternal mortality ratio by 2015

Goal 6. Combat HIV/AIDS, malaria, and other disease
• By 2015 halt and begin to reverse the spread of HIV/AIDS
• By 2015 halt and begin to reverse the incidence of malaria and
  other major diseases

Goal 7. Ensure environmental sustainability
• Integrate the principles of sustainable development into country
  policies and programmes and reverse the loss of environmental
  resources
• Halve by 2015 the proportion of people without sustainable
  access to safe drinking water and basic sanitation
• By 2015 achieve a significant improvement in the lives of at least
  100 million slum dwellers

Goal 8. Create a global partnership for development with targets
for aid, trade, and debt relief
• Develop further an open, rules-based, predictable, and non-
  discriminatory trading and financial system

- Address the special needs of both the least developed countries (LDCs) and of landlocked and small island developing countries
- Deal comprehensively with the debt problems of developing countries through national and international measures in order to make debt sustainable
- In cooperation with developing countries, develop and implement strategies for decent and productive work for youth
- In cooperation with pharmaceutical companies, provide access to affordable essential drugs in developing countries
- In cooperation with the private sector, make available the benefits of new technologies, especially information and communications

Whilst simplicity is a virtue—in particular by making the MDGs relatively comprehensible for non-specialists—it can also be a weakness; and by the very nature of the way in which they were drafted the MDGs inevitably contain compromises and set to one side challenges which have yet to be addressed. The MDG focus on primary education—for example—has in many countries led to the relative neglect of secondary and tertiary education without which the doctors, lawyers, and teachers so essential to the country's development cannot thrive. It is evident on reflection that quality universal primary education is impossible without qualified teachers; or that basic healthcare is impossible without qualified doctors and nurses; or that getting to school or hospital (or indeed getting goods to market) is very difficult without decent infrastructure. Development is indeed a complex business. Few people would in practice now disagree with the proposition that the overall enabling environment must be right for progress to be made against any specific goals and targets.

The dilemma for the architects is demonstrated by comparing the structure of the MDGs with the IDTs. The IDTs had basically proposed three pillars—economic well-being; human development; and environmental sustainability and regeneration (not a million miles from the pillars for a new set of Sustainable Development Goals, or SDGs, to which we will turn later). On the first of these, there was no conflict between the IDTs and the MDGs; there was broad consensus that economic growth was a necessary precondition for economic development, and while the overall goal of halving the proportion of people living in absolute poverty (defined initially as those with income levels below $1 per day, now revised upwards to $1.25 per day) says nothing about the need for growth to be shared equitably there is an assumption that at least some of the benefits of growth will trickle down to the poorest groups to allow the target to be met.

The 'human development' MDGs are also broadly consistent with the IDTs, though with some shifts in language which take out words like equality and empowerment. These are subtle changes, but mean that the focus is primarily on basic needs rather than on rights and equity. The key casualty is the complete omission of the IDT on reproductive health rights and access to family planning. It has been suggested that 'the human development case for reproductive health was challenged by an "unholy alliance" of the Vatican and conservative Islamic states, which managed to get G77 support for their initiative. Consequently, the reproductive health goal disappeared during the negotiations'[3]—though it is worth noting that the MDGs were modified in 2005 to include three new targets, one of them on universal access to reproductive health (the others were on jobs and on universal access to HIV/AIDS treatment), along with a dozen new indicators.[4] Goals 1-6 and the targets and indicators which underpin them have a very sharp focus on specific outcomes in the areas of primary education and basic health to be achieved by 2015.

The third pillar of the IDTs, environmental sustainability and regeneration, is missing almost entirely from the MDGs. Goal 7 is about ensuring environmental sustainability, but compared with the other goals which come before it there is a lack of specific, time-bound objectives in respect of integrating sustainability into country strategies or reversing the loss of environmental resources; and it has certainly not been given the priority accorded to other MDGs. This is in part because at the beginning of the new millennium climate change, in particular, was not yet seen as the threat we now know it to be—a threat not only linked to the environment but also to the achievement of the other MDGs (for example, the likely higher prevalence of vector- and water-borne diseases threatening progress towards the health goals).

But it was also in part because issues to do with the environment were discussed in different forums from international development and, exactly as Mrs Brundtland had feared, the two debates and discussions had become delinked. So the environmental specialists met in their own space, exchanged ideas amongst themselves and attended their own conferences in the same way as did the development specialists; and there was precious little crossing of borders. Where targets for MDG7 were set—such as on safe drinking water, sanitation, and improving conditions for slum dwellers—they were in truth more to do with the achievement of Goal 1 rather than Goal 7, and did not really address broader issues of environmental protection which risked trespassing on the territory of others.

There is one final significant difference between the IDTs and the MDGs,[5] and that is in MDG 8, which calls for a global partnership for development. This was essentially designed to set out what the donor nations would do to support the achievement of the MDGs; without something along these lines the developing countries would most certainly not have signed up to them. But, largely for political reasons, MDG8 lacked the sharp focus and measurable targets of MDGs 1–6. Some of the donor nations (not least those who had declined to sign up to the 0.7 per cent target in 1970) would simply not agree to anything that committed them to specific levels of, or targets for, official development assistance. That battle was left for another day—or rather for a series of international meetings and discussions, beginning in March 2002, which gradually moved the debate forwards.

4

SUPPORTING THE MILLENNIUM DEVELOPMENT GOALS

The Story up to the Global Financial Crisis of 2008

The UN Conference on International Financing for Development took place in Monterrey in Mexico in March 2002. It achieved less than many had hoped, but more than some had thought possible. In practice, it said little specific about additional financing for development, which was the avowed key theme of the conference, simply urging progress towards the 0.7 per cent target and proposing a specific range (0.15 to 0.20 per cent) which should be targeted at least developed countries. This was, however, balanced by specific commitments made at the time by the US and the EU to increase their ODA commitments; and when the conference is considered as a stepping stone following two years of discussion and negotiation, it looks considerably more positive.

As always, it is important to consider the political context. Six months earlier, on 11 September 2001, the world had been shocked by the attack on the twin towers in New York, which had led to a sense in the UN and elsewhere of the need to demonstrate global solidarity in the face of what was perceived to be a growing terrorist threat. It is no coincidence that when US President George W. Bush decided to go to the Monterrey Conference over fifty other heads of state and government made the same decision, along with some two hundred ministers of trade, finance, and foreign affairs.

The conference helped to change the dynamic of the framework within which aid and development were discussed in a number of ways. The communiqué—the 'Monterrey Consensus'[1]—signalled very clearly that recipients of aid had to demonstrate a commitment to sound policies, good governance and the rule of law; but also that development programmes (including their Poverty Reduction Strategy Papers, or PRSPs) had to be 'owned and driven' by developing countries. It commended the development of—and pledged support for—regional development frameworks such as the New Partnership for Africa's Development (NEPAD). And it urged donors to harmonize procedures, such as on the untying of aid (particularly to the least developed countries), leading to substantive discussions in the DAC/OECD over the next two or three years on improving aid coordination and effectiveness, culminating in the 'Paris Declaration on Aid Effectiveness' of March 2005.[2]

The Consensus identifies six areas of 'financing for development', as follows:

- mobilizing domestic financial resources for development;
- mobilizing international resources (such as foreign direct investment and other private flows);
- international trade as an engine for development;
- increasing international financial and technical cooperation for development;
- external debt;
- addressing systemic issues: enhancing the coherence and consistency of the international monetary, financial, and trading systems in support of development.

This all represented progress in the right direction—as did the presence and participation of the private sector and civil society, alongside the Secretary-General of the UN, the President of the World Bank, the Managing Director of the International Monetary Fund and the Director of the World Trade Organization. But there were limits to what could be discussed and what decisions could be made in a forum like this, in particular on trade issues (which were negotiated separately). There was also strong resistance on the part of one or two delegations (in particular in the G8, and specifically the US) to any discussion of 'global public goods', including climate change and the environment, thus reinforcing the separation of these issues from any discussion of international development.

In spite of the language about the ownership of development resting with developing countries, the truth is that real economic and political power remained with the G8 countries. They were the ones who continued to pull most of the levers in the UN system; had a controlling interest on the Boards of the World Bank and IMF; and provided most of the world's concessional resources as well as being home to most of the companies and civil society organizations operating in developing countries. It would require a conscious decision by the G8 to integrate developing country views further into their considerations. To most people's surprise, that is exactly what happened next.

* * *

The G8 summit held in late June 2002 in Kananaskis, Canada, marked something of a departure for these events. These meetings had been held annually since 1976 (the addition of Russia in 1997 turning the Group of Seven, or G7, into the G8; the President of the European Commission had also attended since 1981) and they were intended as an opportunity for the leaders of the world's leading economies to get together in an informal setting to discuss issues of mutual interest and common concern.

The Kananaskis event was the first such summit to have taken place since the events of 9/11, and there was a natural focus on issues such as terrorism and non-proliferation. The summit also covered issues of debt (of concern to many developing countries) and included a 'Market Access Initiative' designed to benefit the forty-eight least developed countries. What really made it different, though, was its specific focus on Africa, in recognition of some signs of progress but also perhaps from a sense that the continent risked being left behind, and that this could have implications not just for making progress towards the MDGs but also for global peace and security.

The key outcome of the Kananaskis Summit was an 'Africa Action Plan' which was designed to be a response to, and provide support for, the New Partnership for Africa's Development (NEPAD) and the new African Union (AU), which had replaced the Organisation for African Unity (OAU). The key founding members of NEPAD—President Mbeki of South Africa, President Obasanjo of Nigeria, President Bouteflika of Algeria, and President Wade of Senegal—were invited to the summit and participated in the discussions of the Africa Action Plan, as did the Secretary-General of the United Nations, Kofi Annan.

The Action Plan picked up and built on some of the key themes which had been discussed at Monterrey. It recognized for example the importance of peace and security, and the need for support for institutional strengthening and governance. At the same time as focusing on trade and economic growth, it also recognized the importance of making progress towards the key development goals of improved health and education.

The Summit saw the creation of 'Africa Personal Representatives', whose role it was to report direct to the relevant G8 president or prime minister on progress towards the commitments set out in the Africa Action Plan. This would be a continuing role, with a specific mandate to report back on progress to the next summit, which was hosted in mid-2003 by the President of France at Evian (following the hosting of a Franco-African Summit in February which had, confusingly, led to the production of a French Action Plan). There was continuing support expressed for NEPAD and for mechanisms such as the Africa Peer Review Mechanism (APRM), a voluntary arrangement under which African countries could submit themselves to an assessment of progress on issues such as the rule of law, democratization, respect for rights, and the independence of the judiciary. In practice, much of the summit was about trying to heal deep divisions within the G8 over the invasion of Iraq.

While all four African leaders who had attended the Kananaskis Summit returned to Evian (with the fifth NEPAD founder member, President Mubarak of Egypt) some other leaders were invited as well, including from China, India, and Brazil. This invitation to a number of the 'emerging economies' to attend was a further significant development—a recognition that the G8 could no longer propose and dispose in the way it had done historically. That shift continued at the 2004 G8 Summit, hosted by the US at Bear Island, Georgia. Four of the NEPAD countries (not including Egypt) attended part of the summit (and the Presidents of Ghana and Uganda also participated), but the focus essentially shifted to issues of global security around the 'broader Middle East', which included Israel and the Arab nations; North Africa; Afghanistan; and Iraq.

How would Tony Blair, the British Prime Minister, decide to position the 2005 UK-hosted summit? Would he continue that shift towards security and away from global economic issues, trade, and development? And where would Africa fit into the mix? In truth, by the time the Bear Island Summit took place, preparations for the UK-hosted summit the following year were already well advanced.

* * *

In late 2003, rock singer Bob Geldof (closely associated with raising awareness of and funds for the Ethiopian famine in 1984–5) called on British Prime Minister Tony Blair to urge him to make development in general and Africa in particular the focus of the 2005 G8 discussions. He suggested that the way to do this would be to create a 'Commission for Africa', which would make an assessment of the state of Africa and come up with a series of recommendations that would form the basis of the G8 discussions and lead to specific commitments.

The proposal had echoes of the commission set up by World Bank President Robert McNamara in 1977 under the leadership of former German Chancellor Willy Brandt (see also chapter 2), which aimed to get around the impasse in North–South negotiations for global development by bringing together key figures in their personal capacity rather than as official representatives of governments or institutions. It was invited to come up with proposals which were 'both essential and possible'.

The Brandt Commission reported at the end of 1979,[3] informed of course by the dynamics of the Cold War. It made no bones about the fact that at its heart lay the need for peace as the precondition for progress—peace not just as an absence of military conflict, but the absence of chaos 'as a result of mass hunger, economic disaster, environmental catastrophes, and terrorism'. Looking forward two decades to the new millennium, its report said there was a real danger that 'a large part of the world's population will still be living in poverty. The world may become overpopulated and will certainly be over-urbanized. Mass starvation and the dangers of destruction may be growing steadily'.

The report also recognized that 'world development is not merely an economic process'. One of the commissioners is quoted as saying that the 'new generations of the world need not only economic solutions, they need ideas to inspire them, hopes to encourage them, and first steps to implement them. They need a belief in man, in human dignity, in basic human rights; a belief in the values of justice, freedom, peace, mutual respect, in love and generosity, in reason rather than force'.

There is a strong link between these principles and the values reflected in the Millennium Declaration agreed in 2000 which gave rise to the MDGs. It was at that summit in New York that Blair described Africa as 'a scar on the conscience of the world'. He saw the potential value of establishing a commission along the lines proposed, a quarter of a century on from the first Brandt Report, where some threats (particularly that of nuclear war as a result of East–West tensions) had receded significantly, but others (particularly international terrorism and environmental destruction) had increased.

Blair took some time to make a decision. He recognized that the impetus generated by the Kananaskis and Evian summits had slowed, not least because the US had largely left Africa off the agenda in 2004. The various commitments that had been made were either taking a long time to deliver or were not being met at all. The G8 and African tracks were not fully integrated. In February 2004 the Commission for Africa (CfA) was launched.

*   *   *

The main purposes of the Commission were to generate new ideas and action for a strong and prosperous Africa, using the 2005 British presidencies of the G8 and European Union as a platform; to support African initiatives such as the African Union and NEPAD; to ensure the implementation of existing international commitments towards Africa; to offer a fresh and positive perception of Africa by challenging unfair and outdated stereotypes; and to listen to African voices.

There were seventeen commissioners, of whom nine were from Africa, seven from the OECD countries, and one from China. Difficult choices had to be made about representation; inevitably some who had a good claim to membership would be left out, and noses would be put out of joint. Whilst the Commission included two Africa Personal Representatives (Michel Camdessus from France and Hilary Benn from the UK), some of the APRs felt that the Commission was undermining their role as guardians of the 'Africa Action Plan' which was designed to support NEPAD. None of the NEPAD leaders was on the Commission, which was in its initial stages treated with great suspicion by the NEPAD secretariat. Of the five Africa regions, neither northern nor central was represented on the Commission.

These potential hurdles were generally overcome, in large part because the commissioners used their contacts and networks to encourage others to buy into the work of the Commission. The NEPAD secretariat was persuaded that the Commission's work would usefully support its own plans. Significant efforts were made to consult civil society in Africa widely as the work of the Commission proceeded. The process worked; but the substance worked well too.

The Report—*Our Common Interest*[4]—was issued in mid-March 2005, and was well received. It provided a compelling development narrative. It asserted that peace and security and reasonable standards of governance were essential preconditions for development. With those in place, it was possible to build the broken and fractured education and health systems that were required to deliver the MDGs. But those systems could not be sustained without strong economic growth, and that required the energy and dynamism of the private sector. Healthy international trade was also crucial for growth, but that was constrained not only by the lack of production of export-quality goods but also by the lack of infrastructure. It noted that the railway and road infrastructure that had been put in place during the colonial era had not been primarily designed to join the continent together but to transport minerals and other raw materials from the interior to the ports for shipping to Europe—a continuing challenge for Africa's development.

There were other forces at work too between the issue of the Report and the G8 summit where decisions would be taken. The Paris Declaration on Aid Effectiveness of March 2005 set out clear principles about country ownership of development programmes, better harmonization among donor programmes, greater use of in-country systems, and mutual accountability. The European Commission produced an Africa Strategy that was entirely consistent with the CfA Report, and a decision taken under the Luxembourg Presidency in May 2005 that the long-standing members of the European Union would meet the 0.7 per cent target by 2015, with new member states committed to 0.33 per cent in the same timetable, helped to create a very positive environment for the G8 summit some weeks later.

Even more importantly, those months also saw the culmination of a massive civil society campaign called 'Make Poverty History' (MPH). The historical impact of such public advocacy (often including celebrity support) has been very significant, at least since the response to television reporting on the Ethiopian famine in 1984, and an important part of the aid dynamic. MPH in many ways represented the apogee of such campaigns in the North demanding action about what was happening in the South, and campaigns ten years on have tended to focus on issues like tax justice which, as we will see, reflect a new focus on global goods (and bads).

MPH focused on three key themes—aid, trade, and debt—which were entirely consistent with the recommendations in the CfA Report. This argued that, if the right conditions were put in place, the international community could and should step up to the plate by liberalizing trade and granting 100 per cent debt relief to the poorest, highly indebted countries, and should significantly increase the flows of official development assistance to Africa, from around $25 billion per annum in 2004/5 to $50 billion by 2010. This doubling of aid was not simply picked out of the air, but was based on carefully costed proposals set out in the Report, focusing in particular on health, education, and infrastructure. And it required no more than that the G8 and other members of the international community should deliver on their existing commitment to the 0.7 per cent target.

It was clear that the recommendations of the CfA Report had to be taken as a whole; it was not a menu from which pieces could be taken selectively. The African Union summit which took place just days before the G8 summit at Gleneagles accepted the Report in its entirety, committing its members to fulfil Africa's side of the bargain. The response at Gleneagles was more mixed. The CfA Report remained the basis of the logic, conclusions, and recommendations in the Gleneagles communiqué, though the Commission itself only got a single reference. The headline objectives on trade liberalization, debt relief, and enhanced aid—the key components of the Make Poverty History campaign—were endorsed. So were many of the other recommendations, though the precise costings which had underpinned them got lost along the way, not least because of the shortage of time for discussion following the London bombings.

The key recommendation which had the most immediate impact was debt relief, implemented through the IMF and World Bank. The forgiveness of debt was linked to policy changes on health and education, and as a direct result millions of children who had previously been unable to go to school were now able to do so—and very quickly. Whilst the doubling of aid to Africa was agreed, in fact only about one half of the increase was actually delivered by G8 countries by 2010. Little progress was made then, or has been made subsequently, on the trade package.

The G8 repeated its aid pledge at the following two summits, St Petersburg in Russia in 2006 and Heiligendamm in Germany in 2007. But at the end of the day the G8 is not the sort of body in which decisions can be enforced—and in practice every G8 member wanted to be free to pursue its own aid and development policies in Africa. There was sufficient consensus to be able to agree broad statements of intent and broad common objectives; but implementation was a different matter, and a number of G8 countries fell significantly short in meeting their commitments.

That shortfall was for a number of reasons, but was in particular because of the global financial crisis in 2008. This led not only to a number of G8 (and other donor countries) not being able to fulfil their aid commitments, but also to the beginnings of a new world order in which the G8 would be of decreasing significance as other countries became more and more powerful economically—and thus less reliant on G8 largesse—and more assertive politically.

5

THE BEGINNINGS OF
A NEW AND LESS
POLARIZED WORLD
ECONOMIC AND
POLITICAL ORDER

The international economic and political changes which had been taking place for some years—the process of globalization—became particularly evident during and in the wake of the global financial crisis of 2008. Those changes were perhaps most obvious in Asia, and above all in China, where the government gradually opened up the economy internally, whilst aiming to keep very tight control politically. The country went through a very rapid period of industrialization, building up a strong manufacturing capability mainly in the east and bringing in cheap labour from the west. The result of this was rapid economic growth, as increasingly high quality products were developed and were produced relatively inexpensively.

Those products—washing machines, electrical appliances, televisions, computers, mobile phones—were very attractive to Western consumers, but also benefited Africa as many of the raw materials required to produce them were exported from there. Even if at that time Africa did not get the benefit of being able to add value to those raw materials, the demand certainly benefited African economies, including during the economic downturn of 2008–9.

In China itself, economic growth achieved staggering figures, averaging between 9.5 and 10 per cent per annum for the first decade and a half of the twenty-first century. Growth at this rate means that the size of the economy doubles over a period of about seven years—so that of the Chinese economy has effectively quadrupled since the beginning of this century, and is now the second largest economy in the world, and fast catching up with the USA. Because of China's (controversial) 'one child' policy the overall population growth in the country has been modest, meaning that the average income has increased substantially. Whilst not everyone has benefited, and China still contains very many poor people living at or below the absolute poverty line, hundreds of millions of people in China have already emerged from poverty in the twenty-first century.

That story has been repeated in other countries in south-east Asia. Vietnam, for example, has made similar progress, with economic decisions being taken largely by government. Economic reforms in the mid-1980s led to the rehabilitation of the country's coffee plant-ations and to Vietnam becoming one of the world's biggest producers. Of course this is not necessarily good news for other coffee producers, like Brazil in Latin America or Tanzania in Africa, not just because of the competition but because a surfeit of a product on the market tends to lead to lower prices.

India has also registered impressive economic growth in recent years, if not as dramatic as China. It has done so under very different economic and political conditions, in the largest (if rather chaotic) democracy in the world, with a global network of entrepreneurs channelling at least some of their resources back to their home country. While China has focused on exporting manufactured goods, India has focused on the export of skills and technology. Although India has lagged substantially behind China's exceptional performance in poverty reduction, hundreds of millions of people in India have also emerged from poverty over the past three decades. To a large extent, this was a result of the more rapid growth generated by economic liberalization that began in the early 1990s—though that growth has also been accompanied by a rapid rise in population.

Both countries have made significant progress towards achieving the MDGs, though particularly in the first few years after the MDGs were agreed they were scarcely acknowledged by those governments as targets to which they aspired. They saw the MDGs as being largely driven and determined by the Western powers, and did not themselves require significant amounts of external donor finance to make their rapid progress from low-income to middle-income status. And while they had both signed up to the Millennium Declaration, they were nervous about a set of goals linked to rights-based language. Nevertheless, in India the MDGs provided a useful backdrop to the impressive progress made in reducing the impact of communicable diseases, and contributed to generating a stronger focus on primary education and thus to large increases in enrolment rates.

Most aid programmes from the G8 and other traditional donors—including the international financial institutions—had conditions attached to them. For organizations like the World Bank and the regional development banks, these conditions focused on economic and social policies. For the bilateral donors they generally also included conditions around respect for rights, pluralism, and democratization. Whilst the Western donors would claim these as universal values, most developing countries saw them primarily as a way for the West to impose its own values on them.

The emergence of China, India, and other developing economies as aid donors (as well as, in some cases, continuing to be aid recipients) created a new aid dynamic, particularly in Africa. African leaders welcomed the Chinese approach, which was to provide packages of grants, concessional loans, mixed credits, and commercial financing without conditionality on human rights or other areas of policy reform. This has caused a great deal of angst amongst the traditional donors, who have felt that their approach has been undermined by the Chinese. African leaders feel that they are, if a few pages behind, at least in the same chapter of development as the Chinese (a view which the Chinese encourage)—though there are emerging concerns within some African governments about the extent to which Chinese assistance programmes are linked to (often successful) efforts to gain access to natural resources. The traditional aid donors are perceived at least to some degree as seeking to impose their own world-view, with the arrogance that that can imply.

What is in no doubt is that the appetite of China to continue to import raw materials from Africa during the financial crisis of 2008–9 protected Africa from the worst effects of global recession—a recession which affected the most advanced economies the worst. The old political and economic order had been shifting for some time; that crisis hastened the shift dramatically.

*　*　*

The global financial crisis (or, as the Chinese prefer to call it, 'the North Atlantic Crisis'), which began in mid-2007 took most people by surprise, and can be attributed largely to the bursting of the housing bubble in the US which led in turn to a stock market crisis in the following year. Whatever the reason, it resulted in what has been described as the worst global financial crisis since the Great Depression of the 1930s, and led to a significant downturn in global economic activity.

Until the financial crisis, global economic growth had been led by the developed countries; during and after the crisis, 'emerging' and 'developing' countries increasingly took on that role. Not all developing countries were immune from the effects of the crisis—some, like Cambodia, were particularly badly affected, and others felt the negative effects of falls in trade, in commodity prices, and in the inflows of remittances (which were in many countries very significant and generally exceeded, by a considerable margin, inflows of ODA). Nevertheless, developing countries fared comparatively much better throughout and after the global economic downturn, and on the whole those that were least integrated into the overall global economy did best.

It was unsurprising, perhaps, that this shift should be reflected in various institutional arrangements. The G20—a group of twenty countries (including the G8) plus the EU—had been meeting at finance minister and central bank governor level since before the advent of the new millennium. President G W Bush decided to call the G20 together at head of state or government level in late 2008 at the White House for what proved to be a new modus operandi, not least because the G20 heads of state or government decided that they would like that forum to continue into the future.

As a result, the G8 has largely given way to the G20 on the international stage. The G8 now tends to make recommendations which are then picked up and taken forward in the G20. As the influence of the G8 has waned, so that of the G20 has waxed. This sounds like a step in the right direction for global economic governance, but in practice the G20 is no more—or less—legitimate than the G8; it is simply a rather larger self-selection. Indeed, in some respects there are fewer opportunities for a number of countries in Africa to express their views and opinions than there had been under at least some of the G8 presidencies, such as those of Canada, France, and the UK in the early years of the twenty-first century (South Africa is the only African member of the G20).

As is perhaps inevitable with a larger grouping, there are many differences of view between the G20 countries on a range of issues, including between those countries which are not members of the G7. So whilst the BRICS (Brazil, Russia, India, China, and South Africa) united in reminding the Australian G20 Presidency in 2014 that it could not take a unilateral decision not to invite Russia to the G20 summit because of its actions in Crimea, the G20 countries between them represent a broad spectrum of opinion. A country like South Korea is at one end of the spectrum, wanting to have a greater voice in decision-making but broadly content with the global economic and political order as it currently exists; India is at the other, having long called for a new international economic order and for UN reforms which would in particular shift power away from the permanent five members of the Security Council.

It comes as no surprise that a set of global institutions and political and economic power structures designed for the world of the mid-1940s should look somewhat outdated in the second decade of the twenty-first century, and that something more root and branch might be required than the occasional adjustment here and tweak there. Even the implicit compact behind the Millennium Development Goals agreed just fifteen years ago (that the developing countries would implement policy reforms which would then be supported financially by the international donor community) looks outdated, as it becomes increasingly difficult to define 'developed' and 'developing' countries, and as a number of countries move from being recipients to donors of aid—or indeed both at the same time.

As those distinctions become increasingly blurred, it becomes evident that countries the world over face a common set of challenges. Some of those challenges—such as climate change and diseases that cross national boundaries—can only be tackled together. Others—such as how to deal with the youth bulge, ageing societies, or problems such as obesity which are the product of increasing global prosperity—are much better addressed on the basis of shared information and a common understanding of the issues. Those types of challenge are now rapidly moving up the international agenda in this brave—and more complex—new world, and we turn to them in chapter 6.

* * *

Even if all of the MDGs were achieved in full, that would—because most of them are relative rather than absolute—still leave hundreds of millions of people living in absolute poverty and millions of children not reaching their fifth birthday. Had success been very limited, there would no doubt have been questions about whether a second generation of goals should be developed. Given the significant progress that has been made, no-one is asking that question; but very many people are asking what a new set of goals might look like.

While the international development community had begun thinking about the post-2015 era in earnest from 2010, when a progress report on the MDGs was considered in the UN, there was no great rush to consider a set of successor goals—not least because of the recognition that this could prove to be a distraction from achieving the existing set. The starting gun was really fired in 2012, when the UN Secretary-General appointed a 'High-Level Panel' (HLP) to report to him in mid-2013 with recommendations about what a new set of goals might look like. The panel was jointly chaired by the presidents of Liberia and Indonesia, and the British prime minister. It comprised political leaders, but also representatives from civil society, the private sector, academia, trades unions, youth, and others. The need to be inclusive and consultative was recognized from the outset.

It was also evident from the outset of the discussion that 'progress' could not be seen as just about increased prosperity, but about social inclusion, equity, and justice. These were all values highlighted in the Millennium Declaration but missing (at least in any explicit way) from the MDGs. Any new set of goals would need to look at the groups who were left out of progress towards the MDGs—in practice, those who for whatever reason were more difficult to reach, including the disadvantaged, the disabled, and the displaced.

And, as suggested earlier, any new set of goals would have to take into account climate change and the environment. It has become increasingly evident that the impact of environmental factors on natural resources and ecosystems, and thereby on the livelihoods and food security of poor people, has in some cases been a barrier to attaining and maintaining the health and education MDGs. Climate change scarcely featured on the international development agenda in 2000; by the second decade of the twenty-first century there was an almost universal recognition not just that it was happening but that it was largely the result of human agency, with huge implications for the sustainability of the planet, notably for agriculture, the availability of potable water, and the prevalence of vector- and waterborne diseases.

Even bringing together the various elements of the environment and climate change agenda will not be straightforward. There is a particular challenge in knitting into a single package the conclusions of the inter-governmental group (thirty countries from five different regions) established after the Rio+20 Conference with the issues arising from the UN Climate Summit (COP20) which took place in

December 2014 in Peru as part of the development of the UN Framework Convention on Climate Change, preparatory to the December 2015 Summit in Paris where (at the time of writing) the aim is to reach a new international climate agreement to replace the Kyoto Protocol of 1997.

All these institutional arrangements are confusing, because of the complex processes involved but also because there are explicit and implicit trade-offs to be made. Above all, these revolve around financing and the interpretation of 'common and differentiated responsibilities', which in shorthand means that developing countries (which hold most of the world's environmental resources) need to take policy measures to preserve them, supported by financial resources from the rich world which will encourage them to do so. That is in itself complicated enough, but there is a reluctance in at least some developed countries to maintain or increase levels of official development assistance if they are going to have to provide large amounts of environmental and climate change financing as well. An alternative in their view would be to allocate all or most of their aid programmes to projects and programmes related to climate change and the environment, which would thus leave very little to support other development priorities. These are issues which will need to be resolved at the third 'Financing for Development' Conference in Addis Ababa in July 2015.

So far, so complicated. When all is said and done, the fundamental challenge remains to bring together issues around poverty, growth, and social inclusion (the traditional purview of the international development community) and those which are about the survival of the planet (which have been the traditional purview of the environment community). The challenge is not so much one of intellectual coherence—Mrs Brundtland had already made the case powerfully—but of institutional structures, rivalries, and trade-offs.

*   *   *

As we have seen, some of the building blocks for the MDGs had been created through agreements reached at UN conferences. One such conference was in Rio de Janeiro in 1992, on the environment. 'Rio +20', a follow-up conference in mid-2012, proposed the establishment of an inter-governmental panel to look at the potential for creating a set of 'Sustainable Development Goals' (SDGs).

This created both an opportunity and a threat. The threat was that the two processes would take on a life of their own, and simply reinforce the divisions between the development and environment groups. The opportunity was of course that they could be brought together, recognizing not only that they are compatible but that they are mutually coherent and reinforcing—sometimes described as 'resilience', elsewhere as 'human security'. An Oxfam discussion paper of 2012,[1] prepared in advance of Rio+20, helpfully conceptualizes this as 'the creation of a safe and just space for humanity', which can only exist by taking into account simultaneously 'planetary boundaries' and 'social boundaries'. So there is a set of issues around environmental degradation, including climate change, loss of biodiversity, and the acidification of the seas, and another set of challenges around rights-based issues like social inclusion, equity, and gender equality. Each set of issues has to be addressed together, as Mrs Brundtland had suggested.

This can be viewed from both ends of the telescope. Environmental degradation and the potential impacts of climate change (rising temperatures, rising sea-levels, the increasing incidence of droughts and floods) are global threats in the medium term but in the short term are already undermining the ability of poor people in poor countries to ensure their food security, health, and access to clean water. At the same time, simply meeting the unmet demand for girls' education and family planning will slow the rate of population growth and (with other policy measures) help to reduce carbon emissions from the levels currently projected.

The High-Level Panel reported[2] at the end of May 2013, getting the integration of the two processes off to the best possible start. It recognized the importance of putting sustainable development at the core of the post-2015 agenda, noting the overwhelming significance of climate change. It concluded—on the basis not only of internal discussions, but of submissions from over 5,000 civil society groups—that the post-2015 agenda was universal, 'offering hope—but also responsibilities—to everyone in the world'. It suggested that it should be driven by five big, 'transformative shifts':

leave no-one behind (ending absolute poverty and hunger for all by 2030);

put sustainable development at the core (integrate economic, social and environmental action);

transform economies for jobs and inclusive growth (creating sustainable livelihoods);

building peace and effective, accountable institutions (good governance, absence of corruption, more transparency);

forging a new global partnership (a new spirit of solidarity and mutual accountability.

The HLP suggested that these five, transformational shifts could, 'at long last, bring together social, economic and environmental issues in a coherent, effective, and sustainable way'.

The HLP could claim legitimacy not just because of the constitution of the panel, with its geographical spread and eclectic mix of skills, but because of the inclusive and transparent process which had been put in place around the panel's work. This process included consultations in nearly a hundred countries, on a number of thematic areas, use of online technology, and the 'My World' survey which sought to identify what sort of issues people believed a new set of goals should target. Those efforts reached over a million people—a small proportion of the world's population, but nevertheless a significant advance on the traditional model of making such decisions.

The UN Secretary-General agreed with the HLP's analysis, describing it in his report of July 2013 to the General Assembly[3] as an important contribution to the process, and picking up many of its proposals. He noted that 'Ours is the first generation with the resources and know-how to end extreme poverty and put our planet on a sustainable course before it is too late'; that 'in a world of great wealth and technological advances, no person anywhere should be left behind'; and that what was required was 'a single, balanced and comprehensive set of goals, universal to all nations, which aims to eradicate all forms of poverty and integrate sustainable development in all its dimensions'.

The Open Working Group on the Sustainable Development Goals, established after the Rio+20 summit, produced its 'Outcome Document' in July 2014 (see Box 4).[4] It achieved a remarkable degree of consensus, largely by accommodating a very wide range of views and opinions in its proposed 17 goals and 169 targets (detailed 'indicators' have yet to be defined). It has achieved the key objective of integrating the 'developmental' and 'environmental' agendas. It makes it clear that 'These goals constitute an integrated, indivisible set of global priorities for sustainable development. Targets are defined as aspirational global targets, with each government setting its own national targets guided by the global level of ambition but taking into account national circumstances.' This neatly finesses the problem of how to include the difficult issues that were ducked by the original set of MDGs, including for example universal access to sexual and reproductive health care services and family planning (a target under proposed goal 3).

*   *   *

In December 2014, the UN Secretary-General issued his own assessment of the post-2015 agenda in his so-called 'Synthesis Report', called *The Road to Dignity by 2030: Ending Poverty, Transforming All Lives and protecting the Planet*.[5] He noted the possibility of maintaining the seventeen goals proposed by the Open Working Group, no doubt recognizing that opening them up to detailed further negotiation would run the risk of losing some key elements of the agreement. Instead, he proposed a sort of superstructure to help frame the goals proposed by the OWG:

Dignity: to end poverty and fight inequalities

People: to ensure healthy lives, knowledge, and the inclusion of women and children

Prosperity: to grow a strong, inclusive and transformative economy

Planet: to protect our ecosystems for all societies and our children

Justice: to promote safe and peaceful societies, and strong institutions

Partnership: to catalyse global solidarity for sustainable development

BOX 4 The Open Working Group Proposal for Sustainable Development Goals

Proposed Goals

Goal 1 End poverty in all its forms everywhere

Goal 2 End hunger, achieve food security and improved nutrition, and promote sustainable agriculture

Goal 3 Ensure healthy lives and promote well-being for all at all ages

Goal 4 Ensure inclusive and equitable quality education and promote life-long learning opportunities for all

Goal 5 Achieve gender equality and empower all women and girls

Goal 6 Ensure availability and sustainable management of water and sanitation for all

Goal 7 Ensure access to affordable, reliable, sustainable and modern energy for all

Goal 8 Promote sustained, inclusive and sustainable economic growth, full and productive employment and decent work for all

Goal 9 Build resilient infrastructure, promote inclusive and sustainable industrialization and foster innovation

Goal 10 Reduce inequality within and among countries

Goal 11 Make cities and human settlements inclusive, safe, resilient and sustainable

Goal 12 Ensure sustainable consumption and production patterns

Goal 13 Take urgent action to combat climate change and its impacts

Goal 14 Conserve and sustainably use the oceans, seas and marine resources for sustainable development

Goal 15 Protect, restore and promote sustainable use of terrestrial ecosystems, sustainably manage forests, combat desertification, and halt and reverse land degradation and halt biodiversity loss

Goal 16 Promote peaceful and inclusive societies for sustainable development, provide access to justice for all and build effective, accountable and inclusive institutions at all levels

Goal 17 Strengthen the means of implementation and revitalize the global partnership for sustainable development

Whatever the final outcome of the discussions in New York in September 2015, and the detailed agreement on a set of post-2015 goals, it is clear that there is a growing determination to end absolute poverty by 2030 and belief that, on the basis of experience with the MDGs, this is achievable. It is also becoming increasingly evident that the goals will be built on three overarching pillars—economic growth, equity, and sustainability. In 2000, growth was associated with the 'developed' countries'; most of them now struggle to attain half the growth rates of many 'developing' countries. Equity is as much an issue for the better-off countries as for the poorer countries. And sustainability, by definition, affects everyone, even if the failure to address it impacts most immediately and heavily on the poorest.

This requires a rethink of notions of 'development' and 'aid'. The implicit compact behind the MDGs was that the developing countries were the ones required to act in order to make progress towards the goals, with financial and technical support from the better-off countries. The proposed new SDGs would require significant action from the developed countries too, for example to 'strengthen prevention and treatment of substance abuse, including narcotic drug abuse and harmful use of alcohol'; 'to halve per capita food waste at the retail and consumer level'; and (in what would amount to a substantial policy commitment) to 'progressively achieve and sustain income growth of the bottom 40% of the population at a rate higher than the national average'. So adoption of the SDGs would require commitments by the better-off countries about their own development paradigm.

The proposed new SDGs unsurprisingly also reiterate the need for the better-off countries 'to implement fully their ODA commitments, including to provide 0.7% of GNI in ODA to developing countries, of which 0.15–0.20% to least-developed countries' as part of the 'global partnership for development' (SDG 17, which builds on MDG 8).

So development is now perceived very explicitly as a universal aspiration which requires action by the developed as well as the developing countries—notions which really belong to a North–South paradigm that looks (and is) increasingly outdated. The drive behind the MDGs came from the donor nations and the international organizations; developing countries and the emerging powers are fully engaged and exerting a powerful influence over the current and future international development agenda. Brazil (supported by other G77 members) has played a key role in building on the Rio and Rio+20 conferences. The Rio+20 outcome document *The Future We Want*, which proposed the establishment of the Open Working Group, also reaffirmed the principle of 'common but differentiated responsibilities'. When that principle was first established in 1992, it clearly put the onus on the developed countries to act on environmental degradation resulting from their primary responsibility for causing it. A quarter of a century on, China and India have joined the USA, the European Union, and Russia as the world's major polluters. It has become increasingly evident that countries the world over face significant common challenges which cannot be addressed purely on a country by country basis, which have the potential to affect the whole global community, and which must be addressed jointly. Welcome to the notion of 'global public goods' (GPGs).

6

JOINING THE DOTS

Global Public Goods and Policy Coherence

'Global public goods' (GPGs) is not a term of particular elegance, but it serves well enough. They are also described as 'commons', in the sense that 'common land' (such as the village green) is owned not by individuals but for the common good of all. So it is in everyone's common interest, for example, that air should be clean and not polluted. Because it moves as a result of changes in atmospheric pressure and wind, it is not possible for people to own air, or to claim credibly that they can pollute their particular piece of air because it will not affect others. Clean, unpolluted air thus clearly qualifies as a global public good.

It is worth making the distinction, perhaps, between the absolute need for concerted international action to address GPGs, and the desirability of concerted international action to address certain other challenges which countries have in common. So climate change belongs to the first category. Child obesity—an increasing problem in many emerging economies—could in theory be addressed on a country by country basis, but doing so successfully is much more likely as a result of the exchange of information and experience.

Many GPGs are linked to the environment in one way or another; and it is often easier to think of their opposite, or 'global public bads', such as pollution of the oceans or the reduction of biodiversity. The one which has the highest profile is undoubtedly climate change. Twenty years ago, the global scientific community recognized that climate change was happening. But it is much more recently that there has been an overwhelming acceptance by scientists—and general acceptance amongst the public—that the primary cause of this change has been the result of human activity, in particular through deforestation and the use of fossil fuels such as coal or oil.

In the short term, global public bads self-evidently can be of enormous (financial) benefit to individuals or communities or countries. An individual who owns oil facilities which pollute, or a community which chops down natural forest to replace it with palm oil, certainly benefits from the exploitation of that resource. And it is important to remember that the development of western economies happened as a result of the shift from agriculture to industry, and that that shift was powered by 'King Coal'.

There are vast reserves of coal in countries like India and China. It is a highly polluting fuel, so it is clearly in the best interest of global society that its use should be minimized. But it is also relatively inexpensive, so those countries have an incentive—if they want to make the swiftest possible transition to an industrial society—to use coal, literally, to fuel their economic growth. Whilst recognizing the polluting effects of coal, they argue—with some justification—that the West did not think twice about polluting the world in the nineteenth and twentieth centuries, so it would penalize them unfairly not to be allowed to use this abundant natural resource.

So GPGs begin to acquire some sort of monetary value. Countries which are rich in fossil fuels might be prepared to exploit them more slowly, for example, if they are compensated for leaving them in the ground. Alternatively, incentives can be given to utilize alternative, cleaner sources of energy such as solar or wind power. Countries rich in natural forests, such as Brazil or the Democratic Republic of Congo, can be encouraged not to allow people to chop down those forests if they are provided with financial incentives to allow them to thrive; those forests are after all the lungs of the world.

So there is clearly a strong case not only for the better-off countries to adapt to climate change themselves, but also to support less well-off countries as they seek to mitigate the harmful effects of past policies for which they have been least responsible but from which they will suffer the most. This means addressing directly issues such as ocean and atmospheric pollution, over-fishing, and deforestation but also providing financial and technical support to developing countries as they seek to implement responsible and sustainable growth policies.

While issues of the environment are the most obvious GPGs, there are other issues too which come into this category, not least in the health sector. It is impossible to control diseases like tuberculosis, HIV/AIDS and malaria without global coordination. Smallpox has been eradicated. Polio is close to being eradicated, but shows worrying signs of reviving in a number of countries where it is impossible to get vaccines to remote areas or where there is strong cultural resistance to their use. Bird flu and the Ebola virus are current and potent reminders of the ability of viruses to mutate and become major killers unless there is strong global coordination to address these challenges.

It is worth remembering, perhaps, that as we commemorate one hundred years since the Great War, history's most lethal influenza virus which began at the end of that conflict flourished and over the following year probably killed fifty and perhaps up to a hundred million people—in any case, a very significant proportion of a world population which then stood at 1.8 billion, a quarter of today's total. That is more than were killed fighting in the First World War; more than have been killed by AIDS in decades; as many in a year as the Black Death killed in a century in the Middle Ages[1]. Unless the world works together to address such issues there is real potential for a modern pandemic to wipe out millions of people from north and south, rich and poor countries alike—especially given the ease of modern travel which can help diseases spread across continents.

However closely countries work together to address issues like HIV/ AIDS and other global health challenges, the responsibility for implementing preventative measures and treatment will rest with national health services; something similar is true in other sectors. Weak institutions and a lack of delivery capability are key blockages to development and poverty reduction, and—as the experience of the Global Alliance on Vaccines and Immunizations (GAVI) and the Global Fund (to fight AIDS, tuberculosis, and malaria) have demonstrated—any enhanced focus on GPGs and global programmes must be accompanied by the building up of delivery capacity at national and local level.

There is a sense in which global security too can be seen as a global public good, so for example it is in everyone's interest that terrorist movements (and the conditions in which their growth thrives) be addressed strongly by the international community as a whole. There is nervousness among some in the traditional development community that an increasing amount of security assistance—to address insecurity across but also within borders—will become classed as ODA. The communique of 16 December 2014 from the DAC High-Level Meeting (HLM)[2] says that: 'Recognising that building peaceful and inclusive societies will be an increasingly important part of the development agenda, we will generate greater political momentum in support of peace-building and state-building efforts.'

Two further points are worth noting from the DAC HLM discussion. First, the point about support for peace-building is linked very specifically to a new statistical measure, with the working title of 'Total Official Support for Sustainable Development' (TOSD), designed to complement rather than replace the ODA measure, and 'to cover the totality of resource flows extended to developing countries and multilateral institutions in support of sustainable development and originating from official sources and interventions'.

Second, in addition to the OECD and accession countries (Colombia and Latvia), the DAC High-Level meeting was attended by observers from Brazil, China, Croatia, India, Indonesia, and South Africa—representing between them over one-third of the world's population—as well as by representatives of the Arab Co-ordinating Group Institutions, the co-chair of the Global Partnership for Effective Development Co-operation (Malawi) and the co-facilitators of the Third International Conference on Financing for Development

(Guyana and Norway). Rather than creating parallel and conflicting systems, there may just remain a possibility of building a global development partnership in which the various actors abide by a common set of standards and rules. We return to that discussion in chapter 7, but for the moment it is worth noting that the TOSD measure is likely to have inter alia the positive effect of ensuring an increasing focus on policy consistency and coherence, to which we now turn.

* * *

Historically, aid has been instrumental in helping countries make development progress, whether in the late 1940 and early 1950s, when US aid played a major role in helping post-war Europe get back on its feet, or in the last years of the twentieth century and early years of the twenty-first, when the international community has supported many countries in trying to make progress towards the IDTs and the MDGs. But in the overall scheme of things aid matters less than it did a quarter of a century ago.

Overall, in 1990 total gross ODA amounted to just over $113 billion, or about a quarter of the total international resource flows to developing countries (which amounted to around $450 billion).[3] And those international resource flows accounted for well over half of total domestic developing country government expenditure of nearly $777 billion. By 2012, total gross ODA had increased by nearly 25 per cent to around $140 billion, but total international resources had more than quadrupled to nearly $2 trillion, and domestic Government expenditure in developing countries had increased eightfold in the same period to over $6.4 trillion.

So overall, aid mattered much less in 2012 than it did in 1990. It mattered less as a proportion of total international resource flows, where it is now outstripped by a very considerable margin by remittances (over twice as much), by foreign direct investment (over three times as much), and by long and short term loans (over four times as much). And it mattered less as a proportion of domestic government expenditure in developing countries, where gross ODA in 2012 represented just 1.7 per cent of gross Government expenditure—a stark contrast with the figure of nearly 15 per cent in 1990.

But it still matters hugely to some countries. In 2012, ODA represented 22.7 per cent of gross government expenditure for least developed countries (LDCs). For low income countries (LICs) it represented 34.8 per cent. So as we move towards 2030 and the target date for the elimination of absolute poverty, it is likely that ODA will continue to focus on helping to get those LICs and LDCs which are successfully setting their own course for their future development across the line, and on getting others—particularly those emerging from conflict and fragile states—as close to the line as possible. So in addition to its role in supporting GPGs, aid will have a crucial continuing bilateral role in many—though a diminishing number—of very poor, vulnerable countries.

There are, of course, many other policies and actions which impact on poorer countries as much or more than aid. It is thus important to have what is known as 'policy coherence' (especially within the European Union) or a 'whole of Government approach' (generally used when referring to bilateral donors), so that other policies do not undermine the development of less well-off countries. This can be illustrated by looking in the first instance at one particular issue, the sale of arms.

* * *

Africa, the continent which is richest of all in terms of natural resources, saw its resource blessing became a resource curse because of poor governance and a lack of peace and security, in turn largely the result of a Cold War in the North being fought as a very hot war in the South, and particularly in Africa. Those conflicts between and within states, particularly in the 1970s and 1980s, were fuelled by weapons imported from outside; with the exception of some limited capacity in South Africa, there is no arms manufacturing capability on the continent.

On peace and security generally, and on the unrestricted selling of, and dealing in, arms in particular there has been substantial progress.

The African Union has significantly increased its willingness to become involved in peace-building and, with international support and in cooperation with the United Nations, its capability to intervene and resolve conflict. There are no active wars between states in Africa, and only limited conflict within countries—though as in other parts of the world Al Qaeda and its affiliates, such as Al-Shabaab in Somalia, are having an impact. All the more reason, then, to invest in development, which is in itself an investment in peace and security.

Discussion on the possibility of creating an arms trade treaty (ATT) to cover issues such as the adoption of effective and legally binding agreements on arms brokering, and common standards of monitoring and enforcement, had been going on since the start of the millennium. In 2013, the ATT was signed by a large number of countries, and entered into force on 24 December 2014 after it had been ratified by the requisite number.

Unrestricted arms sales are just one example of how non-development policies can impact on development, or at least on the conditions required for development to take place. But there are many others, to which we now turn.

* * *

Imagine that you are a cotton farmer in Cote d'Ivoire. You work hard and manage your land efficiently. The road system is beginning to develop so you are able to get your cotton to ports for export. But you find that you are unable to compete on the world market on cost and quality with US cotton farmers. Is this because you are doing things wrong? No—it is because US cotton farmers receive heavy subsidies from their government which allow them to undercut farmers elsewhere.

Imagine instead, then, that you are a cocoa farmer in Ghana. You know that you can get raw cocoa into Europe, but being something of an entrepreneur you decide that you would like to add value to your product by turning the cocoa into chocolates for export. When you look into the possibilities of doing this, however, you discover that the European Union will tax you for adding value to the export commodity (and if you do it using materials sourced from outside the country you may fall foul of the so-called 'rules of origin'), making it quite uneconomic for you to try to add value in this way. That is assuming you can make sense of the rules, which are extraordinarily complex—making them simpler and more transparent would in itself represent a major step in the right direction.

Or imagine that you are a fisherman on the west coast of Africa. You manage to eke out a living and are able to sell sufficient quantities of fish to be able to keep your family and send your children to school. But then European fishing fleets move in and with their mechanized trawlers diminish the fish stocks so that there are simply insufficient to form the basis of a livelihood. At least part of that fishing by commercial fleets from other countries is illegal, unreported, and unregulated.[4]

Or imagine that you are a cattle farmer in southern Africa who is keen to improve the quality of the meat and hides from your herd. Through your government, you receive a grant from the European Development Fund to help you realize that ambition. It appears that nothing can go wrong—until it becomes apparent that a different part of the European Commission has put restrictions in place which forbid the imports of beef and hides into the European Union without fulfilling 'phytosanitary' rules and regulations which would cost you very significant sums of money to comply with.

These are all based on real, actual or historical examples. The international system is full of tariff and non-tariff barriers—including agricultural subsidies—which are designed to protect domestic producers and discourage imports from overseas. These are in many ways a hangover from the old world order and the Cold War period, but in spite of a general recognition that a freer trading system is better and fairer for everyone, once these barriers are in place they are notoriously difficult to remove.

Difficult, but not impossible. Towards the end of the Cold War, expenditure on the European Union's Common Agricultural Policy (CAP) accounted for two-thirds of total EU expenditure, and—because intervention and export subsidies were linked to increasingly large EU agricultural surpluses—did so in a way that particularly distorted international markets. Every European cow was subsidized to the tune of more than $2 per day—twice the amount of $1 per day then used to define the absolute poverty level. As a result of a series of reforms, beginning in 1992, levels of CAP expenditure have stabilized and different types of payment (for example, to encourage rural development and encourage environmental sustainability) are being made, with a substantial reduction in the negative impact on developing countries in general and farmers in the South in particular.

And the draft SDGs are also encouraging in this respect. For example, one of the targets under goal 2 (which is about food security and sustainable agriculture) has as its objective to 'correct and prevent trade restrictions and distortions in world agricultural markets'; under goal 14 (which is about sustainable use of the seas) an end to fisheries subsidies which contribute to overcapacity and overfishing, and to destructive fishing practices, and to provide access of small-scale artisanal fishers to marine resources and markets. There are other areas of policy too which can impact very seriously on the development of poorer countries, and one of the targets under proposed goal 17, which has to do with strengthening the global partnership for development, is specifically to 'enhance policy coherence for development'.

This subject has rightly been a preoccupation for some time of the well-respected Center for Global Development, a think tank based in Washington DC, which produces each year a 'Commitment to Development Index' (CDI) setting out the rankings for the twenty-two countries of the OECD on how they are helping (or hindering) the development of poorer countries, not just or even primarily through their aid programmes, but through other policies.[5]

The CDI looks at a number of indicators and scores the OECD member states against each of the overall indicators, giving them an overall ranking. The indicators include, for example, incentives to invest in developing countries. Particular attention has been paid in recent years to tax policy (including a campaign advocating 'Tax Justice'), and especially to the way in which some major multinational companies have sought to implement tax arrangements that both minimize their liabilities in developed countries and also mean they pay little or no tax in the developing countries in which they are operating or—more usually—from which they are extracting raw materials.

Another area of strong current interest is remittances—funds transferred back to their home countries by the diaspora. These diaspora flows are now over twice as much in total volume as the total aid budgets of the developed countries. The costs of transferring those remittances can vary greatly, one of the key factors being measures put in place by the banking and financial authorities in the developed countries to ensure that the funds are not channelled to terrorism. The comprehensive draft SDGs have something to say on this too, with a target (under the overall goal of reducing inequality within and among countries) of 'by 2030, reduce to less than 3% the transaction costs of migrant remittances and eliminate remittance corridors with costs higher than 5%'. As always, there is a balance to be struck—but it is important that the issues are thought through from all angles, including those of the developing countries.

Other areas looked at under the CDI include environmental policies and technology transfer. Environmental policies clearly matter and, as we have already seen, represent a crucial dimension of GPGs. But the ease of technology transfer can in some cases also be seen as a global public good. Take for example patents which are permitted on medicines. Patents which are too restrictive can prevent the flow of innovations to developing countries—stopping them from manufacturing their own medicines and drugs, for example—and at the same time keep the cost of imported medicines and drugs into those countries very high; what seems to be a rather dry debate about technology and intellectual property rights is in practice, on closer examination, a debate about saving people's lives.

It is thus imperative that aid donors and the international institutions do not measure themselves—nor are measured by others—on the basis of their aid flows alone. It is hard to encourage self-reliance and resilience in developing countries when the international community is to some degree complicit in undermining those very attributes. In practice, it is generally the case that the most generous aid donors also have the best 'policy coherence' or 'whole of government approach' to international development. That will become increasingly evident as we build on the arguments of the previous chapters and ask whether it is possible to discern some emerging trends as we look forward over the next decade and a half.

7

THE NEXT FIFTEEN YEARS

What Might Happen Next in Aid and Development

Some global economic shifts are already well under way and are virtually certain to continue over the coming fifteen years. China will at some stage in the 2020s overtake the United States as the largest economy in the world—even though the pace of growth in China will inevitably slow from current levels in what everyone hopes will be a 'managed landing'. India will not long after that overtake Japan as the world's third largest economy. Because the populations of these countries are several times bigger than either the US or Europe, the average income per capita will of course remain much lower, and will take much longer to catch up.

Continuing substantial economic growth in the most populous countries in Asia (China, India, Indonesia), even if not quite as fast in the second as in the first decade of the twenty-first century, will lead to a sharp reduction in levels of absolute poverty in those countries, building on the significant progress they have already made in the past fifteen years. The emergence of a significant middle class in Asia (by 2030 expected to be as big as the rest of the world combined) will stimulate continued economic growth and a demand for increasingly sophisticated technology and products. A key challenge in those countries will be to accommodate the higher costs of labour and the demands of workers for increased wages without losing their competitive edge. Those demands are likely to include social protection schemes, covering state pensions and other benefits.

In 1990, the baseline year for MDG statistics, over 90 per cent of the world's extreme poor lived in LICs; by 2008, nearly three-quarters of the world's extreme poor lived in MICs. This is largely because a number of former LICs, including a number of countries with very large populations, had moved across the income threshold to become MICs. That statistic should not detract from the progress made in those countries in seeing hundreds of millions of people emerging from extreme poverty. That progress will continue and substantial numbers of people will cross the $1.25 a day poverty line over the coming decade and a half—but they will remain poor. As noted by Sumner and Mallett, 'world poverty is becoming a problem of national rather than international distribution'.[1]

Extreme poverty will be an increasingly African phenomenon: by 2030—assuming that there is significant progress towards the goal of eliminating absolute poverty but that up to 5 per cent of the (much larger) global population could remain below the poverty line—perhaps three-quarters of those living in absolute poverty in the world will be African. There will nevertheless be progress in many African countries, not least as they broaden their economic base away from a strong reliance on primary commodities, and the actual number of people living in absolute poverty in Africa should decline, even though the population in Africa will continue to grow rapidly (and faster than elsewhere) throughout that period.

Does this mean that the ambition of eliminating absolute poverty by 2030 is an unrealistic ambition? As so often, it depends. Deep poverty tends, as we have seen earlier, to be associated with conflict, insecurity, and bad governance; so progress will depend not only on what happens in poor fragile states such as Somalia and Afghanistan but also in middle-income (and populous) fragile states such as Pakistan and Nigeria. How the international community can (and why they should) help in such fragile states is a question addressed later. But progress on getting close to zero absolute poverty by 2030 is inextricably linked with progress on dealing with fragility and conflict.

There are other forces at work too. Globalization has been seen as a generally positive force for development, as long as poor countries are integrated into the global economy; the argument has been that as economic, trading, and investment links strengthen and it is increasingly in the interests of all countries to maintain a peaceful and stable environment to allow those links to develop further, there is a strong disincentive to disrupt that system. Alongside that has been an assumption that multilateral governance arrangements will develop to ensure that that system operates fairly and brings widespread benefits.

That has not happened—and indeed there is evidence that the trend is in the other direction. One reason is that the countries which established the international political and economic governance framework after the Second World War, essentially giving them control of that system, have been reluctant to cede power and make the major adjustments which would reflect more accurately the current situation. The result is that many of the world's economic and political systems and structures remain rooted in the mid-1940s. There has been some adjustment to the relative powers of board members of the IMF and World Bank in recent times, but those institutions remain dominated by North America and Europe. And various attempts to bring about change in the UN system (set out in more detail in Part Two) have made limited progress.

Failure to reform these international organizations risks an increasing degree of marginalization for them. One or two very successful emerging economies—such as South Korea and Mexico—have been broadly content to embrace the Western narrative and find their place within the existing system. South Korea, for example, is a fully paid-up member of the OECD Development Assistance Committee (DAC), and in its aid programmes follows the DAC rules (and it has been very clear that aid was crucial in catalysing its own development process).

A number of the emerging economies have attended recent meetings of the DAC as observers, and are thus engaged in the process of rethinking the measurement of ODA and other official flows of resources. This could raise interesting questions about some contentious issues, like the tying of aid. The untying of aid from the goods and services of the donor country, in favour of competitive procurement, was a major step forward in the discussion of aid effectiveness and value for money, as the costs of procuring those services from wealthy countries was much higher than procuring them from other developing countries. But where those goods and services are available much more cheaply, from countries like India and China, and where the tying of aid could be an important factor in encouraging those countries to participate further in South-South cooperation, the arguments become much more nuanced. In any case, the participation of those countries in thinking through these issues must be to everyone's benefit.

A failure to find some formula about political and economic power-sharing to which everyone can agree—perhaps along the lines of 'common but differentiated responsibilities'—risks further fracturing of the international system. The BRICS (Brazil, Russia, India, China, and South Africa) in particular have become impatient with the status quo, and have begun to create alternative structures or work round rather than with the current arrangements. In mid-2014, for example, they launched a new 'BRICS Bank', intended to fulfil much of the role played to date by the World Bank; China has taken the lead in creating the Asia Infrastructure Investment Bank (AIIB), launched in late 2014. These developments can reasonably be seen, at least in part, as a response to the 'democratic deficit' (a phrase much used by the international community in other contexts) in the governance structures of the IMF and World Bank.

This is not just about a voice within international and multilateral organizations, but also about whether it will be possible to move towards agreement with emerging economies on a broader framework for engaging with developing countries—an understanding that such engagement both by governments and by the private sector should be subject to mutually acceptable norms and values on transparency and corruption, for example, even if not to a set of enforceable rules, thus acting as a restraint on states and businesses seeking to operate outside those norms and values. This would certainly be in the longer-term interests of all parties, but the risk is of course that shorter-term considerations of (for example) easy deals with elites to get access to natural resources will prevail.

There has been an increasing reluctance amongst a number of traditional donors both in Europe and North America to channel resources and influence through existing multilateral and international organizations (even though they carry the most weight in them, and in spite of a broad consensus on how best to address political and economic challenges). They have instead invested in new bodies like the Global Fund (to fight AIDS, tuberculosis and malaria) and the Global Alliance on Vaccines and Immunizations (GAVI). Both of these organizations have a clear and relatively narrow focus—both addressing international health issues—and some donors believe that with clear objectives and a smaller bureaucracy these new bodies can deliver aid more effectively. There is the added attraction of being able to maintain closer control than in other international bodies (financial replenishments are for example negotiated on a voluntary basis rather than on the basis of assessed contributions), thus retaining some of the control of bilateral aid whilst also getting some key benefits of multilateral assistance. Whatever the perceived potential benefits, however, the proliferation of additional institutions inevitably leads to a further fracturing of the international system.

A failure to address the issue of agreeing an international economic and political framework in which all countries can feel they have a stake and can 'own', and which reflects their position in the world, has serious implications. It is crucial—not least for poorer countries—that there should be commonly agreed rules and values around issues like governance, trade, and tax which will encourage investment. There is otherwise a risk of returning to a Cold War dynamic in which natural resources are exploited in ways that bring no benefit to the people of the country from which those resources derive. That can in turn lead to disaffection and (in the absence of a democratic process through which change can be made) an increase in the likelihood of armed opposition and, at the extreme, the growth of terrorist movements able to capitalize on people's sense of exclusion and marginalization; and as we already know insecurity and instability are inimical to economic development.

* * *

So the international community needs to put substantial effort into developing systems of global political and economic governance which are inclusive and which reflect the reality of global power structures in the first half of the twenty-first century, and which can evolve as power continues to shift. This will in turn provide the stable environment and international legal framework structures which will encourage trade and investment and—for example—ensure that the benefits of mineral exploitation find their way to populations at large and not just to political elites. It includes, crucially, governance structures around the management of natural resources, and the development of globally agreed financial mechanisms based on the principle of common but differentiated responsibilities to safeguard the environment on which we all depend.

It is only within such revised structures and systems that the emerging economies will be ready to take on their fair share of addressing global challenges such as climate change, as part of a global coalition in which countries accept mutual but differential obligations. As developing countries make progress and move to middle-income status, they will move away from capital aid support through traditional bilateral donor partnerships and enter into new forms of partnership—and will also be expected to fulfil their share of certain global commitments, reflecting their enhanced economic standing. But they will only be prepared to do so if that standing gives them a proportionate say in decision-making processes.

Even then, success is not assured. Not only is power being dispersed amongst a wider group of nations, it is also being dispersed away from governments, a process accelerated by technological advances. Ideas can now spread around the world in minutes, allowing people to organize themselves almost instantaneously—something which can lead to enormous benefits, of course, but can also lead to vulnerabilities like terrorism and cybercrime. At the end of the day, even if all governments came together with a coherent plan for reform of the international system, the success of global institutions in maintaining global economic and political stability would remain a major challenge.

* * *

At a time when the traditional understanding of what constitutes—for example—'developed' and 'developing' countries is breaking down, is there still likely to be a role for traditional bilateral, country to country aid? And, if so, what form might that support take? It depends. Low income countries (LICs) which are stable are—not least because of the international aid they are receiving—generally on a path to sustainability and graduation to middle income country (MIC) status. Many LICs in Africa (such as Ethiopia) realistically aspire to MIC status by 2025, so there is an expectation that financial aid will continue up to and perhaps somewhat beyond then, but that aid will quite quickly be replaced by private investment capital to finance growth and development. Private capital has a tolerance of poverty, but little tolerance of instability and a lack of functioning legal and financial institutions. And taxpayers in developed countries have little tolerance when aid contributions to MICs substitute for the taxes of the richest people in the MICs, whom they believe should play their part in tackling poverty and inequality in their own countries.

Whilst the need for concessional financial assistance in those countries will decrease over time, particularly as they diversify their economies away from a reliance on primary commodities, and minerals in particular (a position already reached by many MICs), they will have a continuing need for technical support. This could include, for example, help in developing tax systems which ensure that domestic resources are mobilized fairly, in particular from the emerging middle class; social protection policies which ensure that the poorest and most vulnerable groups have access to health care and education; and in the development of democratic institutions which provide the basis of good governance. These mirror closely the needs of the countries of eastern and central Europe following the fall of the Berlin Wall.

This need will not always be met by the traditional donors—there is now a growing number of erstwhile (or indeed continuing) recipients of aid who are beginning to develop their own development assistance programmes. Some of those programmes, notably that of China, are very significant, though difficult to quantify as they do not follow DAC rules and guidelines. Some countries have developed excellent social protection programmes—for example, Brazil's 'Bolsa Familia' programme, which ensures access to health and education for the poorest families, and is a much more relevant model for other emerging economies than longer-established, European models. It is thus encouraging that countries like China and Brazil are beginning to engage with the DAC countries as discussions about new definitions of aid under the rubric of Total Official Support for Sustainable Development (TOSD) begin.

There may also be other areas in which technical support and advice could be useful. The challenges which many poorer countries face include significant increases in population, and in particular in the numbers of very young and very old (both reflecting developmental success); the need to develop higher and further education institutions which will help develop the skills base required for those countries to chart their own development paths; and the shift to cities and towns, including the management and infrastructure challenges that brings. Urbanization is not just a challenge for the developing countries. About 30 per cent—or fewer then one-third of the global population—lived in urban areas in 1950; the figure exceeded 50 per cent for the first time around 2007 and is around 54 per cent in 2015; and by 2050 that figure is expected to be around 66 per cent, or two-thirds of the global population. With the right focus on functioning and productive infrastructure and on making towns and cities pleasant environments in which to work and live, they can be vibrant centres of innovation and employment creation; without that, they will become centres of deprivation and jobless poverty.

Developing countries need to establish their own policy frameworks for addressing these challenges, but there is certainly scope to provide continuing support in these areas—not just through government to government partnerships, but also through civil society links. It need hardly be said that such partnerships can bring significant benefits to both sides.

* * *

That still leaves one significant group of countries which will require continuing and substantial financial support—failed and fragile states, whether they be low or middle income. This is for a number of reasons. First, there is a strong humanitarian motivation to help; many innocent and vulnerable people inevitably get caught up in what is in effect a low-level but ongoing emergency situation, and it is right to give them whatever support is feasible. Second, it is estimated that by 2030 around three-quarters of the world's poorest people will live in failed and fragile states (largely in Africa). Third—and as has become very evident in recent years—armed and violent groups (many of them now operating in the name of religion) are able to use dysfunctional states as a base; and in any event, conflict and insurrection rarely stop precisely at national borders. This can therefore have a very negative impact on both regional and regional stability. Finally, fragile states are in other respects too the weak links in the global system; addressing health pandemics or the trade in illegal drugs also requires global participation.

So in addition to responding to short-term humanitarian disasters caused by, for example, extreme weather events (at least in part a function of climate change), bilateral aid will focus increasingly on fragile, insecure, and badly governed countries which are in danger of being left completely behind. This is expensive and very difficult. Building capacity and institutions from scratch in an insecure environment where there are few safeguards against corruption is not for the faint-hearted and, by definition, those states are the very countries which will not be able to absorb large quantities of external support. It is dangerous, and will require increasing alignment with foreign policy and security objectives—something of which aid agencies (and NGOs) have traditionally steered clear. But to do nothing is ultimately more costly; it is necessary, and requires an integrated, interdisciplinary approach.

This represents in some ways a return to the Cold War model, albeit without the East–West dimension, though the motivation is quite different, and altogether more honourable. It is about finding ways of working with undemocratic and unsavoury regimes which are likely to be more interested in the accrual of personal wealth than in the welfare of their people, pushing the elites in those regimes gradually and fitfully in the direction of greater responsibility and transparency and thereby giving at least some hope of progress to the people of that country, who would otherwise suffer the double whammy of a government that doesn't care and an international community which has turned its back on them. And of course not all the interactions need to be through government; support for NGO and civil society partnerships is an attractive model under these circumstances, though in totalitarian regimes even that can prove very difficult and hazardous for those involved.

It is also, frankly, about having to manage a political environment within which aid is associated with failure. In his very useful chronology of major development events for the fifty years from 1945 to 1995, Helmut Führer[2] refers to the DAC Review of 'Twenty-Five Years of Development Co-operation' in 1985. The review notes that many developing countries had achieved remarkable progress over the past quarter-century and that aid had contributed significantly to those gains. It is, Führer notes, 'in the nature of official development assistance that it is concentrated on countries coping with particularly difficult problems. Official development assistance is not investment banking. It is therefore not directed to the countries with the highest potential investment returns. Aid is ... concentrated in countries with the most difficult and intractable development problems'. In short, if aid doesn't fail from time to time, it is crowding out funding from other, more cautious sources that is designed to make a profit rather than make a difference.

Führer goes on to note that, in spite of this, most developing countries 'have been helped significantly by aid to accelerate social development and to lay at least some of the foundations for rapid economic progress'. That remains the case thirty years on; it has been a hard grind, and it is by no means universal, but aid has become increasingly associated with success. The story has been less about aid being used as a sticking-plaster to deal with chronic failure, and more one of progress which requires continuing aid resources to make sure that progress becomes irreversible. In future a decreasing percentage of overall aid—but an increasing percentage of bilateral aid—is likely to be used to support failed and fragile states, which are failed and fragile precisely because they demonstrate insecurity, or bad governance, or rampant corruption. They are by definition the countries which will continue to need support, and equally by definition the countries where it will be most difficult to demonstrate a positive effect for aid interventions—but which the international community must continue to support if it is to put its hand on its heart and say that it remains determined to deliver on its promise that no-one should be left behind.

*　*　*

It is increasingly clear that international development is not (if it ever was) about 'us' and 'them', but about mutual interest. A healthy, inclusive, and sustainable global economy is good for everyone. So is a world in which everyone has access to decent employment and nutritious food. And so is a world in which capacity can be developed, information shared and action taken to combat threats, whether natural (pandemics) or man-made (terrorism).

The new Sustainable Development Goals (SDGs) have the potential to take us in the right direction. When the Millennium Development Goals (MDGs) were designed, the implicit compact was that the action would need to be taken and the results delivered by the developing countries whilst the role of the more developed countries would be to provide a significant proportion of the external finance needed to make that happen. The SDGs will impose more of a direct responsibility on the developed countries—of course in providing the lion's share of the resources needed to deliver on global public goods, but also (and this is likely to be more sensitive politically) delivering on commitments to make their own societies, as well as those in developing countries, more equitable.

The popular notion of development will become not just about general levels of absolute poverty (a problem of the poorest people in the poorest countries) but of individual levels of relative poverty (a problem of the poorest people in all countries, including the richest). And we need to remember that even if the world is successful in constructing a world free of absolute poverty by 2030, many of the people who have moved across the $1.25 poverty line will remain close to it and be at risk of moving back across the line if they are affected—for example—by a general economic downturn, family illness, or natural disaster. Social protection schemes will need to be in place to ameliorate the worst effects of such events.

'Growth' has been seen as a necessary precondition for 'development' but an altogether riskier proposition for 'the environment'. The three key pillars of the SDGs should encourage us to take another look at these concepts. Gross domestic product (GDP) measures the value of goods and services in the monetized economy, and has been the traditional way of measuring relative wealth and comparative progress. Increased levels of income for poor people and poor communities in developing countries are clearly necessary, but GDP by itself does not tell the whole story. It tells us a lot about economic growth, little about the distribution of the benefits of that growth, and nothing about the depletion and degradation of natural resources which are ultimately the basis of human prosperity.

This was recognized from the very beginning. In 1934, US economist Simon Kuznets appeared before the US Senate as part of their inquiry on how the US was to escape the Great Depression. His specific remit was to advise on how to measure the nation's product-ivity, and he developed the idea of 'Gross Domestic Product', or GDP. Kuznets was himself very clear about what this could measure (aggregate production) and equally clear about what it could not (national welfare). 'Economic welfare cannot be adequately measured unless the personal distribution of income is known', he wrote, and added that 'The welfare of a nation can, therefore, scarcely be inferred from a measurement of national income as defined above'.[3]

Since the Bretton Woods Conference of 1944, GDP has in practice been the main tool for measuring a nation's economy, and has by extension also been used as a proxy measure for the standard of living—something it was not designed to do, as it has nothing to say about the distribution of wealth or indeed other potential indica-tors of development such as access to education and health. This has led to the development of alternative measures of progress, including the UN Human Development Index—which has itself been criticized for taking into account only growth and equity (as defined by access to health and education) and having nothing to say about the environment.

There have been various other ideas about how better to measure economic wealth and progress in ways which take into account natural wealth and social well-being. Natural Capital Accounting is a different way of looking at growth to ensure that the value of natural resources is properly reflected in decision-making; a sort of 'GDP plus' model. Other models recognize economic growth from which ordinary people bene-fit as one element which needs to be taken into account alongside a broader approach to development, such as the multi-faceted poverty and well-being indicators used by the Oxford Poverty and Human Development Initiative. Other measures reject the whole notion that well-being can be measured by any sort of economic indicators and leave them behind altogether; advocates of this view argue that notions of happiness, for example, have little to do with material wealth.

What is already very clear is that ideas about precisely what we mean by 'development', and how we measure it, will be part and parcel of the SDG package. The introduction to the Open Working Group document notes that a 'robust mechanism of implementation review will be essential for the success of the SDGs', and that 'it will be important to improve the availability of and access to data and statistics disaggregated by income, gender, age, race, ethnicity, migratory status, disability, geographic location and other characteristics...There is a need to take urgent steps to improve the quality, coverage and availability of disaggregated data to ensure that no one is left behind.[4]

Notions of North–South are giving way perhaps to the notion of 'solidarity'—a curiously old-fashioned word which has overtones of twentieth century communist philosophy, but which accurately and precisely identifies a recognition of the need to find shared solutions to shared problems in a shared world. But this notion will not really make sense while there is no agreement on global political and economic structures within which to search for those solutions. Failure to reform the existing international institutions risks marginalizing them, as increasingly powerful countries and partners look for ways of working round them rather than working together to make them a proper reflection of the current economic and political balance. Addressing this structural deficit should be a priority.

The global political threats now look very different from fifty or even twenty-five years ago. On the one hand, the risks of nuclear conflict between nation states now look to have greatly diminished (though the potential for political miscalculation means that it cannot be ruled out for as long as nuclear weapons exist). On the other, the risks posed by global terrorism (including cyber-attacks on critical infrastructure, a risk that becomes potentially increasingly serious as technological advances mean that systems are more and more inter-connected) have increased greatly. That certainly requires a coordin-ated international approach to address in the short and medium term—and inclusive development in the longer term, as terrorism and insecurity thrive on poverty, dissatisfaction, and marginalization. There are other risks too, with complex ramifications. A significant fall in the price of oil, for example, has obvious benefits to consumers. But it has serious implications for producers, and can severely damage the economic prospects of countries that largely rely on such commodities. It can shift the balance of global political power and as a result lead to potential instability. And it can undermine the short-term economics of researching and developing alternative, green sources of energy crucial to the future health of the planet.

In this new world, traditional country to country aid programmes will focus on fewer countries, which will in turn call into question the need for self-standing bilateral aid agencies—unless they also have responsibility for coordinating policy coherence. But it is likely that the importance of global foundations and the efforts of individual philanthropists will continue to grow (and need to be reflected in discussions about aid flows; at the moment only NGO and foundation aid which is funded by ODA is included in the DAC/OECD figures). Twenty years ago, their efforts were very marginal; they are now very substantial (the Gates Foundation, for example, has an annual budget similar to that of a medium-sized donor government). At this stage, many of those philanthropists are American or European; there is likely to be a continuing trend towards Asian and African entrepreneurs putting philanthropic funds into their countries and regions.

The private sector, whether large-scale or small-scale, will continue to be a key driving force behind development. Many of the major multinationals now recognize that adding a modicum of 'corporate social responsibility' to their normal operations is not enough, and that they have a responsibility to invest in a sustainable way which benefits local populations at every stage of the supply chain. This is in part self-driven, but also in part because of external pressures to behave in a responsible fashion; the creation of the 'Global Compact' as a UN forum for discussion with the private sector was a significant step.

This leads us to the way in which the world of development has changed most, and is likely to continue to change even faster as we move towards 2030. Better connectivity opens up a whole world of new possibilities for development, for example through mobile banking and remote access to health and education resources, and for aid, through new delivery channels such as internet portals and new instruments for delivering it, through the expanding use of cell phones and the Internet. It will also help in the provision of better data, so that progress against development goals can be assessed more accurately. In this increasingly well-connected world, even in the most repressive societies people know through the international and social media what is going on. This provides a strong imperative for them to demand their own rights and freedoms, and to hold their governments to account.

Largely through technological advances, people now have a voice which they did not have a quarter of a century ago. Through the mobile phone and the Internet ordinary citizens even in the poorest, most fragile countries are able to see more clearly than ever before what is going on in the wider world, often accessing information direct through devices linked to satellite systems, and to express their own views and opinions. These technological changes will only gain momentum over time, reducing the opportunities for interference and censorship.

The number of undemocratic and unaccountable regimes has gradually reduced over the past quarter of a century. That is good for development; it comes as no real surprise to find that aid is less effective in supporting economic growth if political and economic power is held by local elites which have no real concern for the broader population.[5] There is a real prospect that because of better access to information for citizens of fragile and failed states internally—and with support from governments elsewhere in the region, regional organizations and the international community— those decreasing numbers of dysfunctional governments will find themselves under irresistible pressure to reform, however slowly and reluctantly. As the SDGs unfold over the next decade and a half it will be crucial that the rights and freedoms which are both conditions for development and a consequence of it remain firmly at the centre.

At the end of the day—and as Amartya Sen reminds us[6]—development and freedom are inextricably interlinked, even if they do not always proceed at exactly the same pace. Politics is after all ultimately about the relationship between the state and the individual, and how that changes over time. Stability, particularly after a period of conflict, is an important prize, and one for which people are often ready to trade some freedoms, at least in the short term, especially if they feel that their quality of life is improving in at least some areas. In the medium term, though, and as people become better off materially they will also demand more freedoms, to which those governments fail to respond at their peril.

Development is also about capacity. Building the skills and competence of individuals and institutions is a long-term proposition; whatever progress is made towards the SDGs by 2030, that progress needs to be underpinned by stronger capacity. If developing countries and their citizens are to chart their own course, they need to have a functioning legal and judicial system; accountants and auditors; scientific researchers and technical specialists. Africa has around 35 scientists and engineers for every million inhabitants, as compared with around 130 for India; 168 for Brazil; 450 for China; nearly 2,500 for Europe; and over 4,000 for the United States.[7] There is a similar picture in other sectors. The education and health systems which are required to underpin that capacity development (and to provide professional services, including to the poorest groups) themselves need skilled professionals; this will take time to build up (not a year or two, but a generation or two), and is likely to act as a serious constraint to many countries seeking to climb the development ladder. The young professionals of 2030 are already, in 2015, in transition between primary and secondary education institutions, many of which remain understaffed and inadequately funded.

Aid can help to build capacity (not least through better connectivity and the development of partnerships) as well as living standards and conditions, and there have historically been many success stories. It is abundantly clear that the first SDG, of ending extreme poverty, cannot be achieved or sustained without aid. But in the last resort development is about societies making progress as a result of individuals within those societies being able—through the overall environment and through their own innate abilities—to make progress. In spite of powerful reactionary forces, it is increasingly evident that we need to think about society in global terms, having to address common and mutual challenges, whether around growth, equity, or sustainability. In order to do that, we need to rethink many aspects of national and international political and economic governance. That represents a massive challenge; and how we address that challenge over the next fifteen years will be crucial for the well-being—and very possibly the continuing existence—of humankind.

NOTES

Chapter 1

1. Address to Congress by President Harry Truman, 12 March 1947.
2. Department of State Bulletin, 30 January 1949, p. 123.
3. Texts of Truman Orders to Implement Point 1V Plan, *New York Times*, 9 September 1950.
4. United Nations General Assembly, Resolution 3201 (S-VI) 'Declaration on the Establishment of a New International Economic Order', 1 May 1974.
5. Peter Bauer, *Dissent on Development* (Cambridge, MA: Harvard University Press, 1972).
6. Giovanni Andrea Cornia, Richard Jolly, and Frances Stewart (eds), *Adjustment with a Human Face: Protecting the Vulnerable and Promoting Growth* (Oxford: Oxford University Press, 1987).
7. Thomas Pakenham, *The Scramble for Africa* (London: Abacus, 1992). This provides a compelling narrative on the European competition for territory and power in Africa in the late nineteenth and early twentieth centuries.

Chapter 2

1. Independent Commission on International Development Issues, *North–South: A Programme for Survival* (London: Pan Books, 1980).
2. Independent Commission on International Development Issues, *Common Crisis North–South: Cooperation for World Recovery* (London: Pan Books, 1983).
3. World Commission on Environment and Development, *Our Common Future* (Oxford: Oxford University Press, 1987).
4. Carl Sagan, *Pale Blue Dot: A Vision of the Human Future in Space* (New York: Ballantine Books, 1994).

Chapter 3

1. United Nations Millennium Declaration, UN General Assembly Resolution 55/2 of 8 September 2000.

2. Richard Manning, 'Using Indicators to Encourage Development: Learning Lessons from the Millennium Development Goals' (Copenhagen: Danish Institute for International Studies, 2009), p. 13.
3. David Hulme, 'Lessons from the Making of the MDGs: Human Development meets Results-based Management in an Unfair World'. *IDS Bulletin* 41/1 (January 2010): 15–25.
4. See <http://mdgs.un.org> for a full list of the updated goals, targets and indicators effective 15 January 2008.
5. Manning, ibid.

Chapter 4

1. United Nations, *Monterrey Consensus of the International Conference on Financing for Development*: The final text of agreements and commitments adopted at the International Conference on Financing for Development, Monterrey, Mexico, 18–22 March 2002.
2. More details of the Paris Declaration are in Part Two, under 'Aid Effectiveness'.
3. Independent Commission on International Development Issues, *North–South: A Programme for Survival* (London: Pan Books, 1980).
4. Commission for Africa, *Our Common Interest: An Argument* (London: Penguin Books, 2005).

Chapter 5

1. Kate Raworth, *A Safe and Just Space for Humanity* (Oxford: Oxfam, February 2012).
2. United Nations, *A New Global Partnership: Eradicate Poverty and Transform Economies through Sustainable Development*. The Report of the High-Level Panel of Eminent Persons on the Post-2015 Development Agenda (New York: United Nations, 2013).
3. United Nations General Assembly, A/68/202 'A life of dignity for all: accelerating progress towards the Millennium Development Goals and advancing the United Nations development agenda beyond 2015': Report of the Secretary-General (26 July 2013).
4. United Nations General Assembly, A/68/970 'Report of the Open Working Group of the General Assembly on Sustainable Development Goals' (12 August 2014).
5. United Nations, *The Road to Dignity by 2030: Ending Poverty, Transforming All Lives and Protecting the Planet*. Synthesis Report of the Secretary-General on the Post-2015 Agenda (December 2014).

Chapter 6

1. John M. Barry, *The Great Influenza: The Story of the Deadliest Pandemic in History* (New York: Viking Books, 2004).
2. DAC High Level Meeting, 15–16 December 2014, final communiqué, 16 December 2014, <www.oecd.org/dac>.
3. Figures and statistics in this and following paragraphs are based on updated figures from *Investments to End Poverty* (Bristol: Development Initiatives, 2013) and *Improving ODA Allocation for a Post-2015 World* (Development Initiatives, 2015), <www.devinit.org>.
4. The Africa Progress Panel's report *Grain, Fish, Money: Financing Africa's Green and Blue Revolutions* (Geneva: Africa Progess Panel, 2014), provides chapter and verse on the fisheries situation (pp. 87–97).
5. See <www.cgdev.org>.

Chapter 7

1. Andy Sumner and Richard Mallett, *The Future of Foreign Aid: Development Cooperation and the New Geography of Global Poverty*. (Basingstoke: Palgrave Macmillan, 2013).
2. Helmut Führer, *The Story of Official Development Assistance: A History of the Development Assistance Committee and the Development Co-operation Directorate in Dates, Names and Figures* (OCDE/GD(94)67) (Paris: Organisation for Economic Co-operation and Development, 1996).
3. Simon Kuznets, *National Income, 1929–32*. Senate Document 124, 73rd US Congress, 2nd Session (Washington, DC: United States Government Printing Office, 1934), pp. 6, 7.
4. United Nations General Assembly, A/68/970 'Report of the Open Working Group of the General Assembly on Sustainable Development Goals' (12 August 2014), sect. IV paras 14, 17.
5. Luis Angeles and Kyriakos C. Neanidis, 'Aid effectiveness: The Role of the Local Elite', *Journal of Development Economics* 90/1 (2009): 120–34.
6. Amartya Sen, *Development as Freedom* (Oxford: Oxford University Press, 2001).
7. Interview with Dr Alvaro Sobrinho, Chair of Planet Earth Institute, 6 August 2014.

PART TWO

A COMPENDIUM OF KEY WORDS AND CONCEPTS IN AID AND DEVELOPMENT

A COMPENDIUM OF KEY WORDS AND CONCEPTS IN AID AND DEVELOPMENT

As a complement to the narrative account of Part One, this compendium—whilst inevitably being somewhat selective—goes into greater detail about some of the concepts and organizations mentioned previously. There are some common definitions, as in the section on developing country classifications; most disciplines create their own shorthand, language, and acronyms, and the policy and practice of development is no exception. There is more detail on some of the key organizations and institutions (for example, the section on the international financial institutions). And there are some illustrations, such as in the section on security sector reform, of how different elements from within and beyond the development community need to combine in a coherent approach to address particular challenges. The issues are covered under the following general headings:

- Aid Effectiveness
- Capital Aid
- Commonwealth of Nations
- Debt and the HIPC Initiative
- Developing Country Classifications
- Development Assistance Committee (DAC), OECD
- Diaspora

- Food Security and Food Aid
- G7 to G77
- Humanitarian Assistance (Disaster Relief)
- International Financial Institutions (IFIs)
- Non-Governmental Organizations (NGOs), Philanthropists, and Foundations
- Population
- Project and Programme Management: A Glossary
- Security Sector Reform
- Technical Assistance (Technical Cooperation)
- Trade and the World Trade Organization
- United Nations Development System

Aid Effectiveness

Aid effectiveness has to do with how well aid supports the goals of economic and human development, and with making progress towards agreed country or international targets. Measuring effectiveness became a strong priority following the end of the Cold War, when the focus of development assistance became more and more delinked from ideological political objectives (and when judging 'effectiveness' had to a degree to be viewed through the prism of those objectives) and was concentrated more on achieving poverty-related aims. Increasingly, questions were asked about the widespread assumption up to that time that because aid was an additional resource, by definition it made a positive contribution.

Much aid in the 1970s and 1980s worked round rather than with country systems—so for a particular road construction project, for example, a Project Implementation Unit (PIU) might be established, bringing in local 'counterpart' staff who would be trained in the process and could continue once the external funder and technical cooperation staff had withdrawn. This avoided the complications and bureaucracy that might be associated with working with the local transport or roads ministry. That was the theory, anyway—in practice, whilst the project might have been completed more quickly, the local team would often split up on completion, the ministry felt no ownership, its capacity to take on such projects in future had not been improved, and the finance ministry had made no provision in the budget for ongoing maintenance and repairs.

Not only did this model not ensure sustainability, it actually imposed additional burdens on the recipient government as different donors had their own financial and procurement systems which they used for 'their' projects. And as the programmes were then largely run from donor capitals (rather than from in-country offices) there were very frequent and uncoordinated visits which needed to be handled, often overwhelming ministries including (in particular) ministries of finance or planning which were thus unable to get on with their key role of running the country's economic and financial affairs.

The DAC Chairman's Annual Report of 1985, on *Twenty-Five Years of Development Co-operation*,[1] had a good deal to say on the effectiveness of aid, and represented an important step forwards. It noted that 'aid can only be as effective as the policy, economic and administrative environment in which it operates' and that almost as a consequence of this 'in the countries that need aid most, from the point of view of poverty and level of development, results often have been disappointing'. The report also notes the importance of aid helping to create the conditions for its own effectiveness, including building capacity at the local level; the need to support not just individual projects but to take a sector-wide approach taking into account national efforts and policies; and to coordinate more effectively with other donors both in giving advice and supporting projects.

The shift towards greater harmonization and effectiveness, which was a feature of the discussions around the development of the IDTs and MDGs, was given a further boost by the Monterrey Consensus of March 2002. The primary purpose of the Monterrey meeting was on financing for development (to be followed by further meetings on that specific subject in Doha at the end of 2008 and Addis Ababa in mid-2015), but it also inter alia urged donors to harmonize procedures, such as on the untying of aid (that is to say, delinking the goods and services delivered under a country aid programme from the obligation to procure those goods and services from the donor country). This led in turn to a series of meetings, beginning with the Rome High Level Forum on Harmonization of 2003, designed to improve coordination and reduce the administrative burden on recipient countries. That was followed by a meeting in Paris in March 2005, leading to the Paris Declaration on Aid Effectiveness.

The Paris Declaration asserted five key principles, based on partnership. These were *ownership* (it was for developing countries to decide on their policies and programmes, and for donors to support them); *alignment* (the financial and other systems of the recipient country should be used to the extent possible); *harmonization* (donors should avoid duplication and minimize transaction costs by, for example, agreeing on common reporting requirements and standards); *managing for results* (focusing on how programmes would improve the lives of poor people, and developing better tools and systems to measure that); and *mutual accountability* (there should be transparent sharing of information between donors and governments—and more widely—on how funds were used, and their impact).

The Paris meeting was followed three years later, in 2008, by the Accra High Level Forum and then by the fourth and final High Level Forum at Busan in South Korea at the end of 2011. These meetings saw a continuation of the shift towards more developing country involvement in setting the agenda, and more active involvement from foundations and civil society. One key outcome of the Accra meeting was agreement by a number of countries to the International Aid Transparency Initiative (IATI), which set out clearly the standards of openness and transparency to be implemented by signatories. And in Busan there was a recognition of the important role of parliaments and the beginnings of a discussion about South–South cooperation, the role of the emerging economies in general and the BRICs in particular, civil society organizations, and private funds.

The secretariat for the High Level Fora had been provided by the OECD/DAC Working Party on Aid Effectiveness. While they carried out their role very effectively, they necessarily represented the traditional donor group, which created problems for the emerging economies. It was therefore agreed that the High Level Fora should be replaced by a new 'Global Partnership for Effective Development Cooperation' (GPEDC), in which the UN would have a much stronger role (and would alongside the OECD/DAC jointly support the GPEDC). The GPEDC met for the first time in Mexico in April 2014, and agreed that (in line with its name) its focus would shift from 'aid effectiveness' to 'effective development cooperation'. This opened up space for—for example—more detailed discussion of South–South cooperation and triangular cooperation; of global issues affecting rich and poor countries alike such as taxation, illicit financial flows including money-laundering, corruption, and bribery; and the full integration of the private sector, civil society, and other actors into the debate. The communiqué contains a number of annexes reflecting this, including—for example—'Guidelines for Effective Philanthropic Engagement'.[2]

The Steering Committee for the next GPEDC meeting reflects these shifts, and has provision for membership from civil society, foundations, and local government, with the three co-chairs drawn from a traditional donor country (the Netherlands), an emerging economy (Mexico), and a traditional developing country (Malawi). Whilst the major global political and economic institutions do not yet reflect the way the world has changed over the past seventy years, the High Level Fora and now the GPEDC have in the space of little more than a decade shown the flexibility needed to move with—and indeed lead—the times.

Of course none of this will answer those who say that aid doesn't work or, worse, that it positively discourages developing countries from taking tough decisions; that it encourages rent-seeking behaviour; and that nothing done in the OECD/DAC or the High Level Panels or anywhere else really demonstrates that aid has worked. It is though worth noting that probably the most detailed survey of aid ever undertaken, by a team led by Robert Cassen in the mid-1980s, concluded that (in spite of considerable variation, and—an important caveat given the political framework of the time—where developmental objectives were primary) most aid does indeed 'work'.[3] And in a further study carried out within the last decade, Roger Riddell reaches a similar conclusion.[4]

Even the fiercest critics of aid such as Dambisa Moyo[5] (who argues that aid has been a major cause of Africa's problems such as corruption and lack of accountability, but fails to distinguish between cause and effect) exclude humanitarian assistance from their condemnation, and recognize the value of certain interventions (such as support for small-scale enterprise). William Easterly[6] (in a much more nuanced critique, and who makes some strong points about how donors have historically contributed to ineffectiveness through certain approaches) argues strongly that the real blockages to development lie in the imposition of a 'one size fits all' model by development donor ideologues, and that developing countries need to be given the freedom to make their own choices (and mistakes). In that context, he would readily agree that certain interventions—such as reinforcing weak institutions—can make a positive difference.

Equally, the strongest proponents of aid such as Jeff Sachs,[7] who argues that more aid could help poor people and poor countries break out of the poverty trap, readily concede that not all aid works and that it can sometimes have negative effects. So perhaps the middle ground is not so difficult to find after all, and the debate needs to move on to address two key questions. The first should be not whether aid works or not, but under what circumstances it works or doesn't work. And the second should be what constitutes effective development cooperation, and how can its overall impact be measured. The fact that this shift is now under way should be welcome for critics and supporters of aid alike.

Notes

1. Rutherford M. Poats, *Twenty-Five Years of Development Co-operation—A Review: Efforts and Policies of the Development Assistance Committee* (Paris : Organisation for Economic Co-operation and Development, 1985).
2. First High-Level Meeting of the Global Partnership for Effective Development Co-operation: Building Towards an Inclusive Post-2015 Development Agenda. Mexico High Level Meeting Communiqué, 16 April 2014, <www.effectivecooperation.org>.
3. Robert Cassen and Associates, *Does Aid Work? Report to an Intergovernmental Task Force* (Oxford: Clarendon Press, 1986).
4. Roger C. Riddell, *Does Foreign Aid Really Work?* (Oxford: Oxford University Press, 2007).
5. Dambisa Moyo, *Dead Aid: Why Aid is not Working and How There is a Better Way for Africa* (New York: Farrar, Straus and Giroux, 2009).
6. William Easterly, *The White Man's Burden: Why the West's Efforts to Aid the Rest have Done so Much Ill and so Little Good* (New York: Penguin, 2006).
7. Jeffrey D. Sachs, *The End of Poverty: Economic Possibilities for Our Time* (New York: Penguin, 2005).

Capital Aid

Capital aid is the provision of concessional (that is to say, on better than commercial terms) financial resources in support of development objectives. The traditional vehicle for capital aid has been to support specific projects, and is thus referred to as project aid. So support provided to Europe under the Marshall Plan following the Second World War was partly in the form of project aid, in particular to support the rehabilitation of destroyed—or the creation of new— infrastructure such as roads and railways. Most capital aid to developing countries up to and through the 1980s, whether provided bilaterally or multilaterally, was also in the form of project aid. This was partly because much of it was to support the transport, education, and health infrastructure developed during the colonial period, and partly because it was felt that it was easier to ensure that such funds were used for their intended purposes. So if a donor agreed to provide £X to support the building of a school or hospital as part of an agreed cost-sharing plan, and if there was a completed hospital or school at the end of the process, it was reasonable to assume that the funds had been spent as intended.

There are (at least) two potential problems with this approach. If as a finance minister in a developing country I receive £X from a donor to build that school or hospital, I am then able to use that effective saving elsewhere in my budget—either for a very good purpose (such as providing more efficient social services) or for a very bad one (a secret transfer to the military budget). This is known as fungibility. So what initially looks like a tight control of resources is on closer inspection not quite so tight; even if the funds are used entirely for the purposes intended, that transfer releases other funds from the budget which can be utilized elsewhere.

The second downside is that, as a donor, focusing on a particular school or hospital gives me no detailed understanding of the education or health budget as a whole. I can calculate the Economic Rate of Return (ERR) for my investment, and decide whether or not to proceed. But while I have a good deal of information about that particular proposal I may not know much about the funding of the education or health sector as a whole, and still less about the overall country budget, including what provision has been made to protect my investment. There were in the 1970s and 1980s many examples of smart new education and health facilities which deteriorated quickly because there had been no provision within the budget for maintenance—expensive equipment that could not be used for the lack of one or two parts, school classrooms and hospital wards which become unusable because of cracked walls and leaking roofs.

The overall environment has looked rather different since the early 1990s. Governance and transparency have become increasingly important, and as a donor I may well want to focus more of my effort on supporting those areas, which I am likely to do through technical assistance rather than capital aid. Where I continue with capital aid, though, I am ready to make some shift to reflect both the increasing recognition that developing countries must take primary responsibility for their own development strategies and my own wish to understand better the sectors which are key to poverty reduction (particularly health and education).

So rather than just appraising individual projects, I am now ready to provide more general support to sectors—the sector-wide approach, or SWAP. This is referred to as programme aid (as opposed to project aid). I am in a better position to see how, for example, the health sector is financed, and what budgetary provision there is for maintenance and staff salaries as well as buildings. With that knowledge, I am then in a better position to be able to agree to support the government's plans for the health sector more generally, rather than specific interventions within it. In exchange for that broader support, I am able to bring some influence to bear on sector policy, and if necessary can make my support subject to certain policy changes and reforms—known as conditionality.

There is one further consequence of a move away from project support towards programme support, which is that no single donor is likely to be able to provide by themselves, in any aid recipient country, the level of financial assistance required across a major sector such as education or health. This has helped encourage donors into closer collaboration, both among themselves and with the recipient government, in support of a government-owned strategy.

It is of course also possible to provide general support to a country's overall budget rather than to a specific sector or sectors. This is known as direct or general budgetary support. This is only likely to be an attractive option for donors where they have strong confidence in the direction of the recipient government's development programme and in the transparency and accountability of its budgetary procedures. This type of assistance requires continuous dialogue with the finance or the planning ministry, and gives the recipient government considerable flexibility in the detailed use of those resources. In cases where the recipient government is perceived to be falling short of its commitments, donors may elect to move back to supporting specific sectors such as education and health—thus protecting the provision of basic services for the population, but taking away some flexibility from the government in the detailed use of those resources—or may move back to project support.

Most bilateral capital aid is in the form of grants, but some loans (if they are sufficiently 'concessional') also qualify as ODA, subject to rules agreed and enforced through the OECD/DAC. Multilateral aid is generally in the form of loans, and the World Bank and other multilateral development banks generally have two 'windows'. The first of these is a 'hard loan' window (in the case of the World Bank Group, the IBRD), the terms of which are only slightly more concessional, if at all, than market rates. In practice, of course, many developing countries are not sufficiently creditworthy to have access to the markets, so for them this is a crucial bridge between concessional financing and borrowing on the markets. The second is a much more concessional 'soft loan' window (in the case of the World Bank, the IDA), on which only the capital (and perhaps some service charge) needs to be repaid over a very long period of time (25–40 years). This window may also include some grant facility.

One of the continuing problems in spending capital aid entirely on new investments, as was largely the case before 1990, was the lack of funding from recipient governments (because of very limited domestic resources and very low levels of income from taxation) to maintain them, thus diminishing the value of the investment. More recent experience (for example in the health sector) suggests that—particularly for LICs—some provision for the support of recurrent costs (albeit on a tapering basis) alongside capital aid is effective and appropriate.

Commonwealth of Nations

The Commonwealth of Nations—now usually referred to simply as 'The Commonwealth'—has evolved in a way which reflects the changing nature of the international political and economic landscape generally, and the relationship between the United Kingdom and its former colonies specifically.

The 'Imperial Conferences' began in 1911 as discussions between the United Kingdom and its dominions (Australia, New Zealand, Canada, and Newfoundland—then a separate entity which eventually chose to become part of Canada). The dominions were represented separately at the Versailles Conference in July 1919 which finally drew some sort of line under the First World War. The Balfour Declaration issued in London in 1926 noted that the dominions were all 'equal in status' with the United Kingdom, and 'united by a common allegiance to the Crown and freely associated as members of the Commonwealth of Nations'.

The London Summit of 1949 extended this framework to provide for a different sort of relationship between the United Kingdom and many of its former colonies, over and above the Dominions which represented the 'Old Commonwealth', under which all members would be 'free and equal'. When the decolonization process moved into top gear over the succeeding two decades, most of the former colonies became part of the Commonwealth, though some chose to leave and some chose to maintain closer links with the UK and remain 'dependent territories'. Those countries which left included India, which accepted the British sovereign as Head of the Commonwealth in spite of becoming an independent Republic in January 1950—a model followed by many other states, in spite of having their own presidents or indeed monarchies. UK bilateral aid programmes, particularly during the Cold War period, had a strong focus on the developing countries of the Commonwealth.

The Commonwealth became an umbrella for the 'Colombo Plan', a partnership arrangement between the 'Old Commonwealth' donor countries of the UK, Australia, Canada, and New Zealand and the newly independent countries of India, Pakistan, and Ceylon. This was formulated at the meeting of Commonwealth Finance Ministers held in Colombo, Ceylon (now Sri Lanka) in January 1950, and soon expanded to include other donor countries (notably the US and Japan) and recipients (such as Nepal). It was established in part to support regional Governments in countering communism, and adopted a new constitution in 1977 called: 'The Colombo Plan for Cooperative Economic and Social Development in Asia and the Pacific' to reflect its mandate, composition, and activities. The Colombo Plan focused in particular on training and skills development, often through the provision of scholarships. Two of its founder members, the UK and Canada, left the organization in 1991 and 1992 respectively. The Commonwealth Fund for Technical Cooperation (CFTC), as its name suggests, focuses on the provision of technical cooperation across the Commonwealth, with the provision and acceptance of its services being on an entirely voluntary basis.

The Commonwealth itself went through a number of important shifts as it evolved. In line with its mantra that all member states were 'free and equal' it took a strong position on racial equality at its meeting in 1961, which led to the newly created Republic of South Africa withdrawing its application for continuing membership when it became clear that such an application would be unsuccessful. South Africa was readmitted in 1994. Other countries (such as Zimbabwe) have been expelled or have left of their own volition (such as Pakistan), some of them returning after a period of absence.

Because the Commonwealth functions as a voluntary organization—albeit one with fifty-three members, about a third of the world's population, and a quarter of its land mass—it has not found it easy to enforce the principles to which its members have signed up. The Singapore Declaration of 1971 and the Harare Declaration of 1991 both asserted key principles on human rights, freedom, and racial equality to which its members agreed to be bound, but without any legal mechanism to enforce those commitments. So when the Republic of

Rhodesia made its Unilateral Declaration of Independence in November 1965, the imposition of military and economic sanctions was agreed in the UN rather than in the Commonwealth. When the Commonwealth agreed in 1977 to the imposition of sports sanctions on apartheid South Africa, those sanctions were non-binding and were breached on a number of occasions.

As an organization which brings together large and small, land-locked and island, wealthy and poor states, acting as a forum for disparate countries which nevertheless largely share a common language, history, and culture, the Commonwealth is well placed to act as a sounding board for discussions on issues like poverty and development that are also happening in more formal bodies. The Commonwealth Charter of 2013 brings together many key development principles—democracy, good governance, rights, peace, and security. But at the end of the day they depend on the will of individual Commonwealth member states to implement them and to ensure their promulgation in the international bodies that have the mandate and legal powers to enforce them.

Debt and the HIPC Initiative

Countries which are creditworthy have access to the world's capital markets (that is to say, they can borrow funds from commercial banks). The more creditworthy the country, the more it is able to borrow, and the more favourable the interest rate and other conditions which are applied. Moreover, the more creditworthy a country, the less it is likely to need concessional resources; and conversely, the less creditworthy a country is, the more likely it is to need such resources. Sometimes these can get out of balance, as happened in the wake of the oil crisis of 1973–4, when oil prices nearly quadrupled in the space of a year as a result of increases initiated by the Organization of the Petroleum Exporting Countries (OPEC), many of which are in the Middle East, in an attempt to penalize countries in the West (and specifically the US) for their support for Israel in the 1973 Israel–Arab war.

As is often the case, this had unintended consequences. The US in practice produced a very high percentage of its own oil, and the burden of higher prices was borne in large part by non oil-producing poor countries. This was offset to some degree by the willingness of the OPEC countries to provide aid and loans to those countries—some of which undoubtedly had a positive effect, but some of which equally was spent on unproductive expenditure, and in particular arms. This had the effect of ratcheting up debt to unsustainable levels; though whilst the Cold War continued the major powers in the West and the East were ready to support their allies in ensuring that debt arrears did not mount up in a wholly unmanageable way.

Like so many other things, this changed with the end of the Cold War. Newly-elected governments in countries that wished to implement major economic or political reform programmes found that the unmanageable debt burden with which they had been left—debt which had been incurred by previous governments to buy arms, for example, or to prop up the apartheid regime in South Africa—made this impossible. This led to the so-called Heavily Indebted Poor

Countries (HIPC) initiative in 1996. This was designed jointly by the World Bank and IMF to ensure that poor countries (those eligible to borrow from the IDA) were able to manage their debt burden. It has evolved significantly over time.[1] In 1999, a review of the Initiative strengthened the links between debt relief and poverty reduction by making explicit the link between debt relief and the existence of a credible Poverty Reduction Strategy Paper (PRSP).

In 2005, in a year which saw the Commission for Africa, the G8 Gleneagles Summit and the 'Make Poverty History' campaign with its call for progress on aid, debt, and trade, the HIPC initiative was supplemented by the Multilateral Debt Relief Initiative (MDRI) allowing for 100 per cent relief on eligible debts by the World Bank, the IMF and the African Development Fund for countries completing the HIPC initiative process (and in 2007, the Inter-American Development Bank also decided to provide additional debt relief to the five HIPC countries in the Western Hemisphere). The initiative also broadened out to include debt relief from creditor countries, so that approximately half the funding comes from them and half from the international financial institutions.

The agreement on debt at the Gleneagles G8 Summit in 2005, which specifically linked debt cancellation to the poverty targets of the MDGs (as foreshadowed at the Monterrey Financing for Development Conference and G8 Kananaskis Summit in 2002) was the most immediately successful element of the Africa conclusions. It resulted quickly in many children getting admission to primary school and access to health services where this had not previously been the case. Before the HIPC Initiative, eligible countries had on average been spending slightly more on debt service than on health and education combined.

In total thirty-nine countries—thirty-three of them in sub-Saharan Africa—have been eligible for HIPC support. Having fulfilled certain criteria such as establishing a track record of reform and developing a PRSP, they reach the 'Decision Point', at which stage they may receive interim relief on their debt service. After a further period of time following implementation of reform measures, they reach the 'Completion Point', when they receive full and irrevocable HIPC debt reduction. By 2015, debt reduction packages had been implemented for thirty-six of them (thirty-five of them having reached Completion Point and Chad having reached Decision Point), providing over $75 billion of debt-service relief (see Table 1).

Challenges remain. Whilst the major creditors (the IFIs and the so-called 'Paris Club'—an informal grouping of twenty creditor countries, including some of the world's largest economies, with a number of other countries and IFIs as observers) have provided their full share of debt relief, some other bilateral and commercial creditors have delivered only a part of their expected relief or, in some cases, none at all. Because the arrangements are essentially voluntary, there is no legal redress to ensure that the process is completed in a satisfactory manner. And if the remaining countries which have yet to benefit from the scheme—Eritrea, Somalia, and Sudan—become eligible to

Table 1: Post Completion Point Countries

Afghanistan	The Gambia	Mozambique
Benin	Ghana	Nicaragua
Bolivia	Guinea	Niger
Burkina Faso	Guinea-Bissau	Rwanda
Burundi	Guyana	Sao Tome and Principe
Cameroon	Haiti	Senegal
Central African Republic	Honduras	Sierra Leone
Comoros	Liberia	Tanzania
Republic of Congo	Madagascar	Togo
Democratic Republic of Congo	Malawi	Uganda
Cote d'Ivoire	Mali	Zambia
Ethiopia	Mauritania	

do so, additional funding will be required. Nevertheless, the HIPC Initiative has been an important element of the support package for a significant number of poor countries that have demonstrated a commitment to make progress against their poverty objectives.

Note

1. Further details of the HIPC scheme can be found at <www.imf.org/external/np/exr/facts/hipc.htm>.

Developing Country Classifications

The categorization of 'developed' and 'developing' countries began relatively simply following the Second World War, and has become increasingly complicated both because the world has become a more complex place and also because different organizations have come up with different definitions of those and related terms.

It soon became clear that the simple division of the world into 'developed' (basically North America and Europe) and 'developing' (the rest) countries needed to become more nuanced, particularly if there were to be significant transfers of resources from one category to the other. The use of 'LDC' to mean least developed country became increasingly current in the 1960s, and was applied to countries on the basis of three essential criteria—level of poverty (measured as income per capita), level of capacity (institutional and physical infrastructure), and level of vulnerability (stability of economic base and exports).

This category of countries became an accepted definition at the UN in 1971, and four LDC Conferences have been held since then—in Paris in 1981 and 1991, in Brussels in 2001, and in Istanbul in 2011. There are forty-eight countries (mainly African) which fall within the definition of 'LDC'. A goal was set in Istanbul of reducing by half the number of countries falling within the LDC category by 2022; they would then become simply 'developing countries'. This is not straightforward; they are by definition those countries which suffer the most serious structural impediments to sustainable development. There is a UN target, endorsed by the OECD/DAC, of donors committing 0.15–0.20 per cent of their gross national income to LDCs.

We should not forget before leaving this particular classification the very bottom division of the LDCs—the failed states. These are the countries characterized by internal conflict and division, where the reach of whatever central government there is does not extend to the whole country; they lack the infrastructure and wealth to deliver development to their people, such wealth as there is being largely captured by the elites. If the target of halving the number of countries in the LDC category (from forty-eight to twenty-four) by 2022 as they move to middle-income status can be achieved, many of those left will be failed and fragile states, on which bilateral development programmes will increasingly have to focus.

Some classes of country are reckoned to have characteristics which make them particularly vulnerable. Land-locked countries, for example, by definition rely on peace and stability in—and good relations with—neighbouring countries to get their goods to port; and the costs of doing so are in any case higher than they would be if they had port facilities in their own country. Small island states also face challenges of scale and distance to markets. Many of the forty-eight LDCs fall into one or other of these sub-categories, and the ability to graduate from LDC to developing country is particularly challenging. There is even within the UN development system an Office of the High Representative for the Least Developed Countries, Landlocked Developing Countries, and Small Island Developing Countries (OHRLLS) to look out for the interests of these groups.

This notion of 'graduation' is widespread; countries which are eligible for IDA borrowing 'graduate' to borrowing from the IBRD and then again from IBRD eligibility to borrowing on the world markets. This is done over a period of some years, as it is not uncommon for countries eligible for graduation to reach the criteria in one year and then a year or two later fall back; development is rarely a smooth progression. And because there are certain advantages in retaining the LDC label—in particular duty-free and quota-free access to developed country markets—there can actually be a perverse incentive not to seek graduation.

The World Bank Group uses somewhat different categories. On the bottom rung are the Low-Income Countries or 'LICs', broadly equivalent to 'LDCs'. There are then two categories of Middle-Income Countries' or 'MICs'—Lower MICs and Higher MICs—and Higher Income Countries. The LICs are broadly eligible for IDA borrowing; the MICs for IBRD borrowing; and the higher income countries are broadly the donor community. The World Bank is careful to state that this 'classification by incomes does not necessarily reflect developmental status'; some MICs are (confusingly) also LDCs.

There is a plethora of other categories designed to fill some niche or avoid some particular sensitivity. Some countries like Cuba have traditionally refused to recognize even the categories of 'developed' and 'developing', on the grounds that the definitions are essentially those of the 'developed' countries and that there are other paths to development than through industrialization and the promotion of market economies. So sometimes the term 'LEDC' (less economically developed country) has been used to make it clearer that the definition has only to do with GDP and wealth. The UN's 'Human Development Index' uses other criteria such as access to education and health services as a way of looking at development in a more nuanced way.

Other categories which have been used to try to describe categories of country include Emerging Economies or Emerging Market Economies. Another characterization of this group is the Newly Industrialized Countries (NICs)—giving rise to a whole host of new acronyms. So the NICs—rather poetically—include the BRICS (Brazil, Russia, India, China, and South Africa) and the MINTs (Mexico, Indonesia, Nigeria, and Turkey). And in further linguistic acrobatics (and with a degree of overlap with the BRICS and MINTs) there follow the Next Eleven and the CIVETS—all these groups between them filling a number of places at the G20 (see separate entry on 'G7 to G77').

Development Assistance Committee (DAC), OECD

The Development Assistance Committee (DAC) of the Organisation for Economic Cooperation and Development (OECD) was created in 1961. It grew out of the Development Assistance Group (DAG), established in the previous year as part of the Organisation for European Economic Cooperation (OEEC) as a forum for consultations among aid donors on assistance to less-developed countries, a role which it continued under its new name. The mandate of the Committee was essentially 'to consult on the methods for making national resources available for assisting countries and areas in the process of economic development and for expanding and improving the flow of long-term funds and other development assistance to them'.[1]

Many of the key principles set out at this stage continue to inform the discussion over half a century later. There are references to the aspirations of the less-developed countries to improve the standards of living of their peoples; the need to support those countries through different types of assistance, geared to their particular needs; to increase aid volume and to give greater certainty over the timing of flows; and for the 'common aid effort' to focus in particular on concessional assistance in the form of grants or loans on favourable terms. There is a recognition of the need for equitable burden-sharing and stronger coordination of aid programmes—and a need to move away from greater tying of aid.

The DAC soon became a key part of the development architecture, setting standards on aid quantity and quality and playing a major role in following through the UN General Assembly Resolution of 1961 designating the 1960s as 'The United Nations Development Decade'. This included specifically advocating for and monitoring the UN Development Decade commitment to a substantially increased flow of international assistance to the developing countries 'so as to reach as soon as possible approximately 1 per cent of the combined national incomes of the economically advanced nations'.[2] During this period many countries established ministries and agencies with the prime responsibility within those governments for development assistance.

In 1969, the DAC adopted the concept of 'official development assistance' (ODA), separating it from 'Other Official Flows' (OOF), identifying as ODA those transactions primarily intended to promote the economic and social development of developing countries, and which were concessional in character. That was defined as having a certain minimum 'grant element'. And in the same year the DAC Chairman's Report published for the first time figures showing ODA as a percentage of gross national product (GNP)—their total wealth—as a measure of the aid effort of DAC members. This in turn led to a recommendation in the report chaired by a former Canadian Prime Minister, Lester Pearson, called 'Partners in Development' that donor governments should spend 0.7 per cent of their GNP on ODA[3], a target subsequently adopted by the UN General Assembly in 1970 (to be reached 'by the middle of the decade', and proclaiming the Second United Nations Development Decade).

The definition of official development assistance was firmed up in the DAC in 1972, and still remains valid. 'ODA consists of flows to developing countries and multilateral institutions provided by official agencies, including state and local governments, or by their executive agencies, each transaction of which meets the following test: a) it is administered with the promotion of the economic development and welfare of developing countries as its main objective, and b) it is concessional in character and contains a grant element of at least 25 per cent (calculated at a rate of discount of 10 per cent)'. This was set as part of an overall financial terms target for each DAC member's ODA programme of 84 per cent grant element (subsequently increased to 86 per cent).

The DAC in many ways acted as something of a counterpoint to the Cold War dynamic in the 1970s and 1980s, encouraging members to focus their programmes on poverty reduction and meeting basic human needs; to take into account the effect on developing countries of external factors such as the oil price rises of 1973–4; and to ensure that their programmes were as effective as possible (including through better monitoring and evaluation techniques), both through measures such as untying and by coordinating their efforts better. They were particularly supported in these efforts by the Nordic countries who led by example in making progress towards the 0.7 per cent target—Sweden getting there in 1974, the Netherlands in 1975, Norway in 1976, and Denmark in 1978.

The DAC retains a key role in ensuring the quality of aid from (and providing reliable statistics about) the OECD countries, and in setting rules and guidance on—for example—what sort of security assistance can be counted as aid.[4] It has done commendable work on a wide range of crucial issues, including policy coherence; the need to bring developmental and environment issues more closely together; and participatory development, including the role of women. But by its very nature it necessarily excludes many key development actors, and is perceived by the emerging economies in particular as representing the traditional donors—as indeed it does. Like other parts of the international system, the OECD (and the DAC with it) will need to adapt to changing times and become more inclusive if it is not to become marginalized; and the DAC in particular will have to embrace new concepts of international development and broaden its horizons away from an exclusive focus on North–South aid flows if it is to remain relevant in the coming decades. As noted elsewhere, the increasing focus on Total Official Support for Sustainable Development (TOSD), and the engagement with countries like China and Brazil as part of that discussion, represent very encouraging steps in the right direction.

Notes

1. Ministerial Resolution OECD (60)13, 23 July 1960.
2. Helmut Führer, The Story of Official Development Assistance: A History of the Development Assistance Committee and the Development Co-operation Directorate in Dates, Names and Figures (OCDE/GD(94)67) (Paris: Organisation

for Economic Co-operation and Development, 1996). This is an invaluable quarry for information about aid and development from the earliest days until 1993.

3. When the revised system of national accounts was adopted in 1993, the equivalent measure of Gross National Income (GNI) replaced Gross National Product (GNP).

4. 'Is it ODA?' (OECD/DAC Factsheet, Novermber 2008), <www.oecd.org/dac/stats>.

Diaspora

The word 'diaspora' was originally used to describe the expulsion of the Jews from Judaea, and carries with it a sense of forced expulsion from a common homeland and an aspiration to return to that homeland. Other examples include the forced movement of Africans to parts of the Middle East, the Caribbean, and North America as a consequence of the slave trade, and the mass movement of Irish people in the mid-nineteenth century as a consequence of famine.

'Diaspora' has been used more recently to describe groups of people who have been living away from their homeland or continent for extended periods of time. This can sometimes refer to people who may have been forced to leave their country on an involuntary basis but now have no particular wish to return, or to groups who leave voluntarily (and may or may not wish to go back). It is not normally applied to individuals or groups who live away from home for periods of some years for professional reasons—often referred to as 'expatriates'—but the distinctions can become blurred.

Potentially, the diaspora have both money and skills which can be used to benefit their countries of origin, with which they generally retain very close links, and so they can have a very important role to play in international development. The links are perhaps exemplified above all by remittances, the transfer of resources back to the country of origin. These are often to family members who remain in the home country, and can be a crucial source of income—or indeed survival—particularly for those living in failed or fragile states.

This is not always straightforward, and is if anything becoming harder in spite of technological advances which should in theory make such transfers simple. In an effort to crack down on the channels for the transfer of funds to illicit and terrorist organizations, Western governments and banks (under government instruction) have severely narrowed the options for transferring funds to countries like Somalia. This seriously affects the channels for the transfer of resources for legitimate as well as illegitimate reasons, making them either not available or much more expensive—which is more of a deterrent to individuals sending family members a few dollars here and there than to organizations transferring very large amounts of money.

Does it matter? Indeed it does, as the sums involved, even if small when viewed as individual transactions, collectively are enormous. The total value of remittances to all developing countries in 2012 was estimated at over $378 billion, nearly as much as total Foreign Direct Investment (FDI), which was estimated at nearly $490 billion. Both of them exceeded by some margin total gross ODA, estimated at nearly $157 billion. And in that year too remittances represented the largest resource flow to more countries (35) than ODA (34).

The potential contribution of the diaspora is not restricted to funds, of course, but also includes skills. Significant numbers of Africans left the continent during the Cold War period. Most of them have retained strong links with their countries, often through family ties, and as the continent has become increasingly stable and democratic many of them—or their children—are keen to move back to their countries of origin or, in the first instance, at least to strengthen their links. The African Union recognizes the African diaspora as the sixth region of the continent; many countries (such as Ethiopia) are providing incentives such as free land for building residential and commercial property and tax breaks to encourage returnees.

For the international community, supporting the diasporas resident in their countries is an attractive proposition, not only as a channel for funding but also as a key stakeholder group in making decisions about future policy towards the countries concerned. This is not without its challenges. It can be hard to identify diaspora groups who can legitimately claim to represent the interests of a particular community, let alone a country or a continent. And navigating the politics can be complex; many of the diaspora are in other countries because of political differences between them and the ruling party in their home country or region, so supporting them can lead to charges of political interference in internal politics.

A particular challenge now emerging is the radicalization of a very small minority of diaspora in countries in Europe and North America who are—through encouraging and participating in sectarian conflict in their countries or regions of origin—helping to create conditions in which sustainable and inclusive development becomes increasingly difficult to achieve. That poses direct as well as indirect threats to the peace and stability of the world as a whole—not just the risks of terrorist acts taking place (as they have done) in Europe and North America, but a risk of countries and communities in those regions turning inwards, with a growth in nationalist parties and suspicion of all things 'foreign'. This is in no one's interest, and the diaspora can play an important role in contributing positively to their adopted societies as well as maintaining links with their homelands.

Food Security and Food Aid

The goal of global food security is the provision of nutritious, afford-able food for all in a way that can be sustained. This sounds like a relatively straightforward proposition, but in practice is enormously complex and needs to be addressed at many different political, eco-nomic, and technical levels—and to take into account exponential increases in the global population (see separate section).

Access to food and water have been historical drivers of develop-ment, their absence (or, in the case of water, sometimes too much) a major cause of death and an incentive to migration. The ability to bring food to where people were, through cultivation and farming, rather than having to hunt or forage for it, has lain behind the creation of settlements, towns, and cities for ten thousand years, spreading out from Mesopotamia into Egypt and Europe. In ancient Mexico, farmers domesticated teosinte—the ancestor of maize—nine thousand years ago. These developments were accompanied by water management techniques, ranging from large-scale dams and canals to farm ponds. Sophisticated large-scale agricultural and animal husbandry combined with infrastructure development, and in particular methods of bulk transportation, were an essential pre-condition for the industrial revo-lution in Europe and elsewhere in the eighteenth and nineteenth centuries.

In many parts of the developing world, particularly Asia and Africa, agriculture in the middle of the twentieth century looked remarkably like agriculture centuries or even millennia earlier—a precarious sub-sistence existence at the mercy of the elements, natural disaster and human conflict (see section on Humanitarian Aid). In the early 1960s, indeed, China was suffering from famine and India was thought to be on the brink of starvation. But the importation of improved varieties of maize, wheat and rice led to the 'Green Revolution', raising global yields of all three crops massively, particularly in Asia, where cereal production doubled between 1970 and 1990, outpacing population growth.

Whilst the introduction of new varieties lay at the heart of the Green Revolution, other important factors were also at play. Governments gave political support. New capital resources were attracted into farming, which became increasingly efficient (including a significant reduction in post-harvest losses through, for example, managing insect infestation) and mechanized. The use of fertilizer—which was not suitable for some of the more traditional varieties—became widespread, and the infrastructure developed which allowed that to happen.

This revolution has not yet taken hold in much of Africa, and there is in many areas significant potential to use land more productively with existing and affordable technologies (such as different seed varieties, more efficient water management, and use of fertilizer). So by 2030 much of Africa could have significantly increased agricultural production, providing food for a rapidly growing population, giving employment opportunities, and saving on large food import bills.

Are hunger and famine then things of the past? Clearly not—as is evident from the news almost every day, the risks remain very real, particularly in countries and regions where there is conflict. In spite of the impressive record of the Green Revolution, the benefits have been primarily felt in Asia rather than Africa. There is evidence that some of the yields from the Green Revolution are beginning to fall, as pests and diseases have taken their toll. Scientists are busy developing new varieties which will respond to particular circumstances—too much or too little water, for example. And this research has the potential to throw up varieties which can have their nutritional capacity boosted and which can thrive in poor conditions and on degraded land, where the poorest groups of people tend to live.

There is a continuing debate about the potential for GMOs (genetically modified organisms) to meet the needs just described. It is possible to modify genetically rice and other grains so that they can provide additional vitamins. There is no evidence that GMO food poses any greater risk to humans than other food, and it has considerable potential to respond to particular conditions, or to be a vehicle for the delivery of certain vitamins and nutrients. Much of the produce of the US—corn, soybeans, cotton—is GMO food. There is, though, continuing resistance to its spread, for a number of reasons—safety, environmental concerns, and economics (many GMOs are subject to intellectual property rights, often owned by private sector companies). The debate continues...

Even with continuing technical advances, producing food for a rapidly growing global human population is a huge challenge—Malthus (see separate section on 'Population') believed it was a fallacy to think that agricultural improvements could expand without limit, and even with the development of new technologies he must be right. Much of the best agricultural land is being converted into buildings and roads as new cities develop (and population growth of course also increases pressure on forests and other natural resources, putting biodiversity at risk). Global warming is likely to have a negative impact on food production, pushing down yields. Water—particularly on the large scale needed for rice production—will become more scarce, and rising sea-levels and increased salinity will affect rice grown in river deltas. Changes in dietary preferences mean that there will be a demand for more meat, which needs more land and leads to greater emissions, thereby stimulating the vicious circle of climate change and its negative impact on food production.

Given the fundamental importance of food to human survival, it comes as no surprise to learn that food aid has historically been an important aid instrument (in the US it is known as PL480, as its provision is made under that particular Public Law). It is entirely appropriate as an emergency response to disasters, but deeply flawed as a form of long-term development assistance, as it tends to have the effect of undercutting the price of food grown locally and acts as a disincentive to local farmers and entrepreneurs. In practice, and particularly during the 1970s and 1980s, it was used as a means of hitting a dual target of mopping up agricultural surpluses created by heavy subsidies to farmers in the north (particularly North America and Europe) and counting the value against the 0.7 per cent aid target.

Following the end of the Cold War, and after the European agricultural reforms of 1992, food aid as a long-term development tool diminished significantly, and is now used essentially to respond to humanitarian situations. Where possible, it is now purchased in country or within the region in order to minimize distortions. Food for work programmes give food in exchange for work. This work is often linked to maintaining the rural road infrastructure, for example, and sometimes beneficiaries receive cash rather than food so that they are able to purchase food of their own choice. In both cases, the link to food grown locally means that the local economy benefits.

As Narayan reminds us in *Voices of the Poor*, poverty is multidimensional and 'consists of many interlocked dimensions. Although poverty is rarely about the lack of only one thing, the bottom line is always hunger – the lack of food.'[1]

Note

1. Deepa Narayan, *Voices of the Poor: Can Anyone Hear Us?* (New York: Oxford University Press, for the World Bank, 2000), Introduction, p. 4.

G7 TO G77

The history of international relations reflects a patchwork of short-term and long-term alliances formed in pursuit of common economic and political objectives. Some of them have evolved over time to reflect a changing world; others remain stuck in a historical time-warp. All of them can claim some legitimacy; all of them have been criticized for being unrepresentative.

The 'Group of 77' (G77) was created in mid-1964, and was designed to provide a forum for those countries which were not members of the OECD, the Council of Europe, or the USSR. It now has 133 members and a subgroup known as the G24 or, to give it its full title, the Intergovernmental Group of Twenty-Four in International Monetary Affairs and Development. It meets twice a year around the Annual and Spring meetings of the IMF and World Bank, and has Secretariat support from the IMF. All members of the G77 may, without being formal members of the G24, join its discussions.

The Non-Aligned Movement or NAM was created in 1961, and had its first meeting in Belgrade. It has 120 members and 17 observers, and there is a strong overlap between its membership and that of the G77 (with whom it had a number of joint committees). Its purpose was to provide a forum for UN member states who were not part of the Eastern or Western bloc—though in practice many of its members were aligned with one side or the other. It struggled to manage internal conflicts between its members (such as India and Pakistan or Iraq and Iran), and fractured at the time of the Soviet Union's invasion of Afghanistan in 1979 as the invasion was strongly supported by some member countries and equally strongly opposed by others.

A number of leading members of the G77 and NAM pressed very hard through the 1970s and early 1980s for the establishment of a New International Economic Order or NIEO. This was largely done through the United Nations Conference on Trade and Development (UNCTAD), and was designed both to bring about a more favourable trade regime but more fundamentally to challenge the primacy of the Bretton Woods Institutions. The main discussion forum for the first set of issues has moved to the World Trade Organization (WTO). The composition of the boards of the IMF and World Bank are somewhat more representative than they were; but the real shifting power balance is more evident elsewhere.

The G5 (France, Germany, Japan, the UK, and the US) was created in the early 1970s essentially as a forum for finance ministers and central bank governors to discuss the global economic situation and a coordinated response to global shocks (such as the oil crisis in 1973). Italy became a member in 1975 to make it the G6, and Canada followed the next year so that it became the G7. President Yeltsin of Russia was invited to participate in G7 meetings from the early 1990s—when it became known as the G7+1, and Russia formally joined the group in 1998 so that it became the G8. Russia was suspended from the G8 in March 2014 following its annexation of Crimea; this was temporary, but as at early 2015 the suspension remained in place.

In parallel with continuing discussions in the G8—which became an increasingly important forum covering both economic and political issues for heads of state and government, as well as for continuing discussions at a more technical level—it became clear that there was a need for a forum to promote dialogue between the major industrial and emerging market economies. Thus was born the Group of Twenty or G20 in 1999 (though unsurprisingly it had a predecessor in the G33, which in turn succeeded the G22). It had its first meeting at Head of Government level in 2008, in response to the global financial crisis, and since then has effectively taken on greater power as the G8 has lost it.

It is easy to challenge the legitimacy of any of these 'G' and associated groups, which are essentially self-appointed and self-selecting. There are potential advantages to having groups which bring together broadly like-minded countries in a relatively informal way, but they tend to become increasingly formalized with the passage of time. And, like more formal bodies such as the UN or the Bretton Woods

Institutions, they need to move with the times. The G8, for example, has supported some valuable initiatives (not least the agreement on the widespread cancellation of multilateral and bilateral debt at the UK-hosted G8 Summit at Gleneagles in 2005). But any group claiming to represent the world's major economies which did not include China (in particular—but others too like Brazil and South Korea) began to look increasingly anachronistic, and the ascendancy of the G20 is certainly a step in the right direction.

That said, it is not entirely self-evident that countries which were excluded from the G8 and which continue to be excluded by the G20 will be any less marginalized than before. It will be important to ensure not only that major international bodies like the UN, IMF, and World Bank continue to reform to reflect the changing balance of world economic and political power, but also that more informal structures and groupings too reflect the importance of the less powerful countries having a voice.

Humanitarian Assistance (Disaster Relief)

Most aid is designed to support the medium and long-term development prospects of recipient countries. Humanitarian aid—also known as emergency aid or disaster relief—is intended to respond to short-term humanitarian crises, and specifically to save lives and to alleviate suffering. These crises are often caused by natural phenomena (typically weather events or geological upheaval such as flooding, hurricanes, or earthquakes). They may also be the result of human action, often conflict and insecurity but sometimes catastrophic failures of infrastructure (such as the collapse of bridges or buildings or the breakdown of nuclear facilities).

These crises are of course not confined to the developing world. Africa—which carries more than its fair share of disasters and the burden of the world's diseases—has over the past 150 years been practically untouched by hurricanes, typhoons, and other major storms, which have been particularly ferocious along the eastern seaboard of the United States and in the Caribbean, East Asia, and the Pacific. On the whole, though, countries like the US and Japan are able to respond effectively by themselves to such crises because they have the financial and infrastructure resources to do so; developing countries do not.

There is a whole international system for responding to emergencies and disasters, which is loosely linked to—but largely separate from—the institutional structures of the international development system. Three major organizations or types of organization are involved. First, there is the United Nations: within the UN system the UN Office for the Coordination of Humanitarian Affairs (UN OCHA) leads on the response to emergencies and disasters. Other key UN bodies include the World Food Programme (WFP), created in 1961 to provide food aid in response to famine, natural disasters, and armed conflict, and the Office of the United Nations High Commissioner for Refugees (UNHCR), established in 1950, which works to protect the rights of refugees, asylum seekers, and stateless people.

Second, there is the International Committee of the Red Cross (ICRC), which was established in 1863 with the basic mission of ensuring ethical treatment for wounded belligerents in conflict situations, and was responsible for the adoption of the first Geneva Convention in 1864, codifying those rules. Its specific mandate, within a framework of strict neutrality, remains to protect the victims of international and national armed conflicts, which can also extend to the coordination of international relief efforts.

Third, there are Non-Governmental Organizations (NGOs). Many of the major international NGOs in fact started life supporting the rebuilding of Europe during or at the end of the Second World War. So CARE began life as the Cooperative for American Remittances to Europe, providing food aid to Europe before shifting its focus (and its name—to the Cooperative for Assistance and Relief Everywhere—though it is always known by its acronym) to the relief of poverty globally. Oxfam began life as the Oxford Committee for Famine Relief in 1942, focusing initially on famine relief in Belgium and Greece, then providing food parcels to Germany from 1945. Both of them, and many others, have then evolved into global organizations with an increasingly long-term development focus, but with a continuing emergency and humanitarian capability. The international NGOs have shifted away from implementing projects themselves through the provision of a full package of finance and expertise, and they now work more closely with local partner CSOs by providing them with the financial resources to carry out the work, thus ensuring much stronger local ownership and importantly increasing the prospects for short-term emergency support becoming longer-term.

The Disasters Emergency Committee (DEC) is a consortium of UK major international development NGOs (including Oxfam and CARE), set up in 1963, which takes decisions about whether and when to launch an emergency appeal in response to a specific crisis. Even though the bulk of the work of many of those NGOs is in supporting longer-term development, their humanitarian work often has a higher profile (not least because it is more heavily covered by the media). One unfortunate consequence of this is that 'aid' can become associated with disasters and emergencies rather than with support for long-term development and, by extension, with failure and suffering rather than with success and progress.

Nevertheless, the number of disasters precipitated or heightened by conflict (often with ethnic or religious roots) shows no signs of diminishing. Conflict makes the provision of support to those affected much more difficult and dangerous. Even where there is no military dimension (but even more so when there is), responding to emergencies and humanitarian situations is enormously complex and, if it is to be effective, requires the best possible coordination between international and local actors. On those occasions where external military intervention is required in response to a particular humanitarian situation—and particularly if this involves actual fighting—it is crucial that there should be a continuum of activity between the short-term logistical tasks and longer-term development priorities, turning the shock of disaster into permanent societal and democratic gains (often as part of a security sector reform programme—see separate entry).

It is likely that the number of disasters caused by natural events (albeit exacerbated by human activity) such as flooding and the consequences of rising sea-levels will if anything increase. This has led to a recognition of the need for greater 'disaster preparation and preparedness' and the need to anticipate future problems, for example by better training and the pre-positioning of emergency supplies. A global Humanitarian Leadership Academy was launched in March 2015 to develop local capacity to respond immediately to crises. However successful the world is at making progress towards the Sustainable Development Goals, and in particular in getting people across the absolute poverty line, there will regrettably always be a risk of people being pushed back across it by emergencies and disasters—which is why there will be a continuing need for a swift and effective humanitarian response capability.

International Financial Institutions (IFIs)

The Bretton Woods Institutions (the IMF and the International Bank for Reconstruction and Development, or World Bank) were established at the end of the Second World War. A number of additions were made to the World Bank in subsequent years. The International Finance Corporation (IFC) was created in 1956, with a remit to advance economic development by supporting the private sector to undertake projects that will reduce poverty—'to further economic development by encouraging the growth of productive private enterprise in member countries, particularly in the less developed areas'. The IFC is able to support such projects either through loans or through equity participation.

The International Development Association (IDA) was created in 1960. It was designed to support the poorest countries—those with the lowest per capita incomes which because of low creditworthiness were unable to borrow on the capital markets. It remains the largest international provider of funds to support economic and human development projects in the world's poorest countries. Unlike the IBRD, which raises funds on the capital markets, it is funded through regular replenishments (every three years) from the donor countries. The IDA has traditionally made 'soft loans' or 'credits', with long grace periods before repayment has to begin; long maturities (between twenty-five and forty years); and with low interest rates. Loan repayments have meant that the IDA has now effectively become a revolving fund, with repayments being lent out again as new transactions.

There is now some provision for the IDA to make grants as well as soft loans. When IDA countries reach a certain level of wealth (updated annually, and set at $1,195 per capita per annum in fiscal year 2013) they 'graduate' to IBRD lending. Countries also graduate from the IBRD; this process is triggered by reaching a certain income level (currently $6,725 per capita, per annum), but other factors such as institutional capability and creditworthiness are taken into account before any decision is implemented.

The International Centre for Settlement of Investment Disputes (ICSID) was created in 1966, with a mandate to provide facilities for conciliation and arbitration of international investment disputes between foreign investors and host states (it also researches and publishes on international arbitration and foreign investment law). The final constituent body of the World Bank Group was established in 1988 with the creation of the Multilateral Investment Guarantee Agency (MIGA), which provides political risk insurance or guarantees to promote foreign direct investment into developing countries.

The World Bank is also referred to as a 'Multilateral Development Bank' (MDB). A number of other MDBs—or Regional Development Banks (RDBs)—were created over the same period. The first of these, in 1959, was the Inter-American Development Bank (IADB), with its headquarters in Washington DC. The African Development Bank (AFDB) followed in 1964, headquartered in Abidjan (though because of conflict in Cote d'Ivoire it moved for a period of time to Tunis, only completing its move back to Abidjan at the end of 2014). The Asian Development Bank (ADB) was created in 1966, and is based in Manila, in the Philippines. Within Africa, the African Development Bank is in practice usually referred to as the ADB.

These MDBs all follow a similar pattern to the World Bank Group, with a facility for lending to the better-off member-states on quasi-commercial terms and a more concessional facility for the less creditworthy, poorer countries. Thus, for example, the African Development Fund was created in 1972 as part of the African Development Bank group to cater for the poorer member countries. As with the World Bank, the institution reports to a resident board of directors (and ultimately to governors, who are usually ministers of finance) who represent both the borrowing countries (referred to in the case of the RDBs as regional members) and the donor community (the non-regional members). As with the World Bank group, the RDBs raise funds for their lending operations on the capital markets, and their more concessional resources are the result of regular replenishment negotiations.

The picture is completed by the European Bank for Reconstruction and Development (EBRD), created in 1991. This was designed to provide support for the private sector in the newly-democratizing countries of eastern and central Europe following the end of the Cold War, and now lends in a range of countries from central Europe to central Asia. It has also developed programmes in countries in North Africa and the Middle East (specifically Egypt, Jordan, Morocco, and Tunisia) following the Arab Spring of 2010–11, and these countries are expected to become full members of the EBRD in the near future.

Non-Governmental Organizations (NGOs), Foundations, and Philanthropists

Most aid activities are carried out by governments (as recipients or donors) or by inter-governmental bodies (like the UN, the World Bank or the Regional Development Banks). But there is a crucial role played by non-governmental organizations (NGOs) too.

NGOs come in all shapes and sizes, and finding a definition which includes all of them is not straightforward. They are, by definition, separate from government—but can be funded by governments (or by the private sector, foundations, or individuals). Some of them may be run entirely by volunteers; others are highly professional bodies with salaried staff, but most rely on support from volunteers to some degree. They can range in size from one or two volunteers working at community level with a tiny budget to organizations with an annual turnover of hundreds of millions of pounds and thousands of paid staff working at national and international level. They are not-for-profit, and in the UK and elsewhere often have charitable status.

From its earliest stages, the UN recognized the need for some specialized international NGOs (focusing, for example, on international development or environmental or human rights issues) to be involved in their deliberations, and they were given observer status at assemblies and other meetings. This trend has continued: for example, at meetings of the UN General Assembly there are in addition to the formal discussions a series of events for NGOs—both the international NGOs (INGOs), and organizations from the 'global south'. These latter tend to be referred to as Civil Society Organizations (CSOs).

Many international NGOs have a capability of supporting both emergency, humanitarian work and activities with a long-term development focus. In addition to implementing projects and raising funds, many NGOs engage in significant advocacy activities (in practice often closely linked to fundraising), either as individual agencies (often around a single issue such as malaria or clean water) or as part of a coordinated campaign around a broader set of issues such as the 'Make Poverty History' Campaign of 2005. It was massively successful, but was the product of a world which was still viewed very much through a North–South prism. New campaigns—such as the Tax Justice Network—tend to reflect a more integrated world, where there are common issues which have to be addressed on a global basis. The 'Action/2015' Campaign is a global coalition of NGOs seeking progress in particular at the New York meetings in September 2015 (on the SDGs) and Paris meetings in December 2015 (on the environment).

Organizationally, too, international NGOs have had to respond to a rapidly changing world. They have done this in a number of ways. First, there are few large INGOs which do not now have a broad base of support beyond the country in which they were founded. So organizations like CARE and Oxfam, Save the Children, and WaterAid now tend to have, in addition to a national board in their country of origin, a number of other national boards in other countries, with their overall strategy and policies determined by an international board on which the national boards are represented. Second, their in-country operations, in which the senior management teams used to be largely expatriate, are now run mainly by nationals of the country in which the activities are taking place (which is a trend in the in-country staffing of official aid agencies too). Some such as ActionAid have gone further and deliberately shifted their centre of gravity from North to South (in ActionAid's case moving their international head-quarters from the UK to South Africa).

As governments in 'the South' become generally better equipped to provide services like education and health, the need for NGOs to provide similar services should reduce; and in many ways the NGOs face the same challenges as donor governments in knowing what, if anything, they should be doing to support development in middle-income countries. Of course there will still be work for them to do working with poorer and marginalized groups, which will include not just project support activities but also advocating on their behalf. This may be welcomed by the government of the country concerned, but equally it may be resisted and could even become dangerous—particularly if those NGOs are in some way associated with (or perceived as being a front for) opposition politicians.

INGOs are likely to have a continuing, important role in failed or fragile states, working either through a strong local office or in partnership with other local NGOs. In those countries, citizens face the challenge of a government that cannot or will not provide them with the services to which they should be entitled, in an environment within which it is difficult for official aid agencies to operate and come to their help. Local civil society organizations—with the necessary financial backing from outside—are able to help provide those basic services.

There is also potential, in stable developing countries, to develop civil society partnerships across the board—not just international NGOs with local NGOs, but trades union with trades union, fire service with fire service, municipal authority with municipal authority, school with school, and so on. These partnerships create a two-way learning process from which everyone benefits; it is a more equitable model of partnership for what should become a more equitable world, in which the old North–South distinction becomes, as it should, a matter of historical interest rather than a way of proceeding.

Many NGOs raise a majority of their funds from the public, but may get some of their resources from governments (which may count as ODA). They may also get some from trusts and foundations, which use their wealth—often that of individuals, sometimes of institutions and organizations—to promote causes of welfare or social justice. Most trusts and foundations are essentially funders, largely of NGOs, and generally have no operational capacity to implement projects or programmes themselves.

It may be said that at the heart of government and the non-governmental sector lies the concept of public initiatives for the public good; at the heart of the private sector lies the concept of private initiatives for private good (though increasingly companies allocate at least some resources to Corporate Social Responsibility, or CSR); and at the heart of philanthropy and the work of charitable foundations lies the concept of private initiatives for public good. Much of this effort was—and still is—conducted at national level, so (for example) the Peabody Trust created in 1862 in the UK was and remains concerned with the provision of housing for the poor, whilst in the US there is strong philanthropic tradition in the education sector.

The links between philanthropists on the one hand and international aid and development on the other are long-standing. In 1863 Henry Dunant, a Swiss businessman, founded the Geneva Society for Public Welfare, which became the International Committee of the Red Cross (ICRC), a key actor still in many humanitarian situations. In the US the Ford and Rockefeller Foundations supported work both in the US and internationally; but in spite of their generosity and that of many smaller foundations, philanthropy in support of international development remained a comparatively modest endeavour in the twentieth century.

That changed at the turn of the twenty-first century, when the Bill and Melinda Gates Foundation (BMGF) was established, with an overall mission of reducing global poverty and in particular supporting the provision of healthcare. Their own contribution has been more than matched by another US philanthropist, Warren Buffett, who has contributed $31 billion to the Foundation (of which he is a trustee), giving it the ability to make grants worth several billion dollars each year—as much as a medium-sized government donor. Because they have had a very strong focus on vaccines and immunizations, they have become a very significant player in that area. Other philanthropists have focused on other areas (George Soros, for example, has created the Open Society Institute, OSI; Chris Hohn and Jamie Cooper Hohn the Children's Investment Fund Foundation, CIFF).

There has also been a notable increase in home-grown philanthropy in countries like India, South Africa, and Nigeria, with very successful entrepreneurs and businessmen like Ashish Dharon, Mark Shuttleworth, and Aliko Dangote putting part of their wealth back into their own countries to support—for example—education or health interventions. This is a continuation of the tradition of figures like Joseph Rowntree and Andrew Carnegie in the UK and US in the nineteenth century, and one which now—as then—has the potential to make a significant contribution in the fight for social justice and against poverty, and to underpin the future role and voice of civil society.

Population

Thomas Malthus's *Essay on the Principle of Population* (1798)[1] suggested that increases in population exceeded the power of the earth to produce sufficient food to feed the global population. If 'epidemics, pestilence and plague' failed to keep populations in check, 'gigantic inevitable famine' would follow until populations reached the level at which they could be sustained by the available food resources. Catastrophe was not inevitable, though the effects of 'the great law of necessity which prevents population from increasing in any country beyond the food which it can either acquire or produce' would inevitably cause disproportionate hardship and suffering amongst the poorest sections of the population.

When Malthus wrote his *Essay*, the world's population stood at around one billion people. It took until around 1920 for it to double to two billion. It reached three billion by 1960, and the rate of increase in the global population reached a peak in 1971, when it was growing at a rate of 2.1 per cent per annum. Extrapolations done at the time suggested that continued compound growth at that rate would mean that by around AD 3200 there would be too many people physically to fit on the surface of the earth. Such compound projections of course do not recognize that human behaviour and technological solutions can adjust to take account of changing situations. They should be treated with the same sort of caution as the prediction in *The Times* in 1894 that, as a result of the increase in horse transport across the city, every street in London would be buried beneath nine feet of horse manure by 1950 (the technological solution in that case being the advent of the car and tram). In truth, there has been since 1971 a slowing down in the rate of increase in population growth rates (albeit not yet in the number of people).

There is nevertheless cause for concern. Since 1960 the world population has more than doubled again to over 7.2 billion. Current estimates suggest that it is likely to increase to somewhat over nine billion by 2050 and could then stabilize at around ten billion by the end of the 21st Century. There are more pessimistic scenarios, with the rise going to eleven billion by 2050 and continuing beyond that; but even more modest increases will put significant pressures on the planet's ecosystems. Those pressures include the increasing use of fossil fuels and the resulting environmental degradation, as well as the significant impact on biodiversity—the increasing dominance of the human species has led to the extinction or potential extinction of many other life forms. Forty per cent of the planet's surface is now being used for agriculture, directly destroying (or making untenable through the use of chemical pesticides) the habitat on which other species depend.

People have traditionally had large families in the expectation that many of their children would not survive into adulthood; it was a rational insurance policy in the face of disease, famine, and war and the lack of health and medical facilities. And there were limited means for parents, and women in particular, to achieve smaller family sizes, especially in the absence of contraception. In the 'developed' world, better access to health care and contraception has meant that family sizes have decreased significantly as a conscious choice—to the extent that some countries such as Italy and Japan have concerns that there will be insufficient people of working age to generate the wealth to look after the older generation. It has been estimated that simply by meeting the unmet need for family planning, population growth will slow to the extent that globally carbon emissions will be reduced by between 8 and 15 per cent—the equivalent of stopping all deforestation immediately.[2] This is a good example of the interconnectedness of issues affecting humankind and the future of the planet.

Population growth is not just about increasing numbers of young people surviving into adulthood; it is also about people all over the world living longer than before. This means that there is both a youth bulge (half the population of Africa is aged 18 or less) and an age bulge. These are development successes, largely the result of a widespread, significant increase in access to healthcare, preventive medicine and treatment, and as such are to be celebrated. There are consequences which need to be recognized, however. Whilst people are often living longer as a result of treatment previously unavailable, they may not be able to look after themselves and will often require continuing care and medication—with both social and economic consequences. If you live in a country where average life expectancy is forty-five, it may not make a great deal of difference if there is no social protection or old age pension scheme to be accessed at the age of sixty or sixty-five (especially as those surviving to that age are likely to come from more privileged backgrounds). But if life expectancy increases to seventy-five, it matters a great deal.

The other thing that is likely to matter a great deal to you is whether or not you have a job. There is—rightly—a good deal of emphasis on the importance of an education system which leads through from primary school to secondary school, with the potential then for going into a job or undertaking further training which will develop job-related skills. But it is also crucial at the other end of the spectrum—as people live for longer and have a reasonable expectation that part of that increased lifespan will be when they are fit and healthy, they need to be able to continue longer in employment to sustain themselves and their families, particularly if there is no social protection scheme in place.

Changes in circumstance take time to work through into behaviour change; social attitudes often take a while adjust to new realities. So even when people know that there is every chance of all or most of their children surviving into adulthood, the default position remains to take no chances and continue to have large families. That is assuming they are permitted to do so, of course—with its 'one child' policy, China's population of around 1.4 billion people (nearly 20 per cent of the global population) is significantly smaller than it would otherwise have been. It is growing at a rate of around 0.6 per cent a year (the same sort of rate as is typical in Europe). The population of India, the second most populous country in the world, is growing at around 1.25 per cent a year. These numbers contrast starkly with Africa, where the typical figure in population growth is somewhere between 2.5 and 3.5 per cent per annum, with an expected doubling of Africa's population from one to two billion by 2050.

Even in Africa, though, the significant increase in the numbers of girls going to school (educating girls is widely recognized as one of the most effective development interventions) and better access to family planning means that rates of population growth will slow as family sizes shrink, though these changes will take time to work through and be reflected in the population growth statistics. Whatever the final figure for Africa, and for the world more generally, it is abundantly clear that the planet cannot sustain current consumption patterns typical of Western countries. The richest 7 per cent of the global population account for half of all carbon emissions; the poorest three billion people account for 7 per cent of those emissions. As we know from Oxfam's 2014 Equality Report,[3] the richest eighty-five people in the world have the same wealth as the poorest half—3.6 billion—of the world's population. A growing global middle-class aspires to a life-style which includes—for example—access to personal transport and more meat in their diet, both of which have consequences for sustainability. If prosperity is to be measured by increased economic growth alone, then global aspirations and population growth are on a collision course. Something will need to give in the process.

And something more might need to give. Sometimes technology and innovation can surprise everyone, for good or bad. Just suppose that a pharmaceutical company, addressing the challenge of old age as a disease to be treated rather than an inevitable consequence of life, discovered a means of ensuring that most if not all people could live to be a hundred years old, or even more. The consequences would be very significant. The global population would clearly undergo a substantial increase with major effects on planetary pressures, but there would also be huge implications for family life (for example, if five or six generations of a family found that they had to live together), for health and social care systems, for the relationship between those in employment and those for whom they were responsible. This may seem like a vanishingly small prospect; but the truth is that a number of pharmaceutical companies are working on this very issue, and within the period covered by the SDGs the consequences of a scientific breakthrough might need to be addressed as a development issue with global implications.

Notes

1. Thomas Malthus, *An Essay on the Principle of Population.* (1798; Oxford: Oxford University Press, 1993), Chapter VII.
2. Kavita N. Ramdas, *What's Good for Women is Good for the Planet.* (Washington, DC: Aspen Global Health and Development, October 2010).
3. Oxfam, *Even It Up: Time to End Extreme Inequality.* (Oxford: Oxfam, October 2014).

Project and Programme Management: A Glossary

Like all disciplines, aid and international development have their own language and vocabulary, which can sometimes be difficult to follow for those coming to the subject for the first time. This section is designed to shed a little light on some of the common terminology used by specialists.

First, let us turn to the various stages of the project cycle, as seen from a donor perspective. A project or programme is a series of connected activities designed to bring about clearly specified objectives within a defined time period and budget. Project Cycle Management is used to describe the various policy and management stages from the inception to completion of a project or programme. These stages are sequential, with each phase providing the foundation for the next. They are as follows:

- *Identification*: Finding a project or programme which looks as if it might be viable, and which fits within the priorities agreed between donor and recipient;
- *Preparation*: The next phase, involving the detailed design of the project, including making some sort of cost–benefit analysis. This is largely a technical process;
- *Appraisal*: This looks in detail at (for example) the potential gender, institutional, and environmental dimensions of the proposal. This may include consultation with local stakeholders (those involved with or who may be affected, positively or negatively, by the potential project or programme);
- *Approval*: This involves getting agreement to the project or programme as a whole, including the financial plan and phasing of disbursements;
- *Implementation*: This is the carrying out of the project or programme, normally over a period of some years.
- *Monitoring*: This is to ensure that that activities and financing remain on track and in line with the original plan. Monitoring is

essentially an internal process designed to check on progress of the activity and to take any required actions to get it back on track or to adjust the timetable or activities should circumstances require.

- *Evaluation*: This is an assessment of how well the project or programme has performed against its objectives, with the key intention of drawing lessons for the future. It is normally undertaken at the end of a project or programme (though it is also possible to have one or more interim evaluations), often by an external body to ensure objectivity.

One tool which has been developed to help pull together the various elements of this process is the 'Logical Framework' or 'Log-Frame'. This is designed to be used throughout the project cycle, and to ensure greater clarity on overall objectives, purpose, and desired results, together with indicators on how the objectives, purpose, and results can be measured. Those indicators are sometimes defined more closely as 'Objectively Verifiable Indicators' or 'OVIs'.

In a further refinement, these OVIs are designed to be SMART:

Specific to the objective;
Measurable;
Available at acceptable cost;
Relevant to information needs; and
Time-bound.

Whilst Logframes allow information to be analysed and organized in a standard way—which is good in itself, and certainly helps the harmonization process between different actors if used widely—they can if used too mechanically become a burden rather than a help, and a bar to constructive thinking rather than a support. As Professor Bob Picciotto, a former Director of the World Bank Operations and Evaluation Department and one of the world's leading evaluation experts, has wryly observed: 'To be approximately right is better than to be precisely wrong'.[1]

This harmonization process has also led to agreement on how certain terms in the project cycle should be used, such as *input, output, outcome* and *impact*. These can perhaps be best illustrated by an example. The government and donor community decide that they need to address the problem of poor teaching in schools. The *inputs* are the overall financial and training resources provided by the government and international community to address the problem. The *outputs* are the numbers of teachers who have been trained and skills have been improved as a direct result of these interventions. The *outcomes* are (for example) the number of children who are being better taught as a result. And the *impact* is a longer-term measure showing, for example, how the economy has grown as a result of better-educated children entering the labour market.

Note

1. Robert Picciotto, 'The Evaluation of Policy Coherence for Development', *Evaluation* 11/3 (July 2005): 311–30.

Security Sector Reform

Security Sector Reform (SSR) is of particular interest because it integrates a series of processes—of which aid may constitute a part—that go to the heart of the creation of a functioning state, bringing together concepts like peace and security, development, and rights.

The notion of SSR was first widely used to describe the route by which the various actors in the security sector—the military, intelligence agencies, police, the judiciary—in the emerging democracies of Eastern Europe in the early 1990s moved from being unaccountable controllers of the political process, often operating beyond the law, to becoming servants of the State and protectors of the rights of individuals.

In other countries, and particularly in Africa, there was often a prior step in the process, which was stabilization—the bringing to an end of conflict between ideologically opposed military forces. This could be the result of internal negotiations, often involved external mediation, and occasionally included external military intervention or peacekeeping. Once stabilization had been achieved (a process which, as is evident from the example of Afghanistan, could take many decades), the next step was often the disarmament, demobilization, and reintegration (DDR) of any armed forces within the country but outside its official armed services. Those official armed services, once they no longer had to deal with internal conflict, were themselves often downsized.

Whilst operations such as peacekeeping (which had and can have a significant developmental value) are not fully counted as aid, support for DDR is, and in countries like Uganda in the early 1990s there was significant international support for the process. That then led into the early stages of the SSR process, which often began with military-to-military training, with the objective not just of improving military professionalism but of explaining how this fitted with the broader responsibility of the military to the elected government of the day, within a clear framework of rules and rights. Like peacekeeping, capacity-building in the military could not be counted in full as aid, but as the armed forces tended to become smaller and more efficient there was also a parallel effort—fully supported by aid programmes—to develop the civil law enforcement agencies, and specifically the police. In autocratic regimes, supported by the military (and indeed frequently in practice military regimes), the police were often marginalized and undisciplined, attracting a reputation for being both inefficient and corrupt, and abusers rather than the protectors of human rights.

There are many other parts of the jigsaw that need to be addressed. For the police to perform their role efficiently there has to be a trusted judicial system with impartial judges and lawyers able to prosecute and defend cases. This requires capacity—not only the physical capacity of buildings to constitute an efficient courts system but also and more importantly human capacity, so that there are people trained to an adequate standard at every level in the system—judges and lawyers at one end of the spectrum, drivers and clerks at the other. It requires an efficient, transparent, and well-managed prison service, a well-regulated border management system, and a fully accountable customs service.

It is also important that there should be proper democratic control of the intelligence agencies. Whilst they undoubtedly have a crucial role to perform in protecting the state from external and internal threats, there is a fine line between the need to keep some of their activities outside the public domain and the danger that they could become unaccountable—and in some cases (including within at least some of the G8 countries) they have operated on the wrong side of that line. This in turn argues for the need to have a system of parliamentary democracy which is able to hold the intelligence services to account whilst at the same time preserving the integrity of necessarily classified information.

All these potential areas of improvement are premised on the fact that states wish to reform their security sectors and that they are content to work with the international community in doing so. This was evidently the case in many countries in eastern and central Europe after the end of the Cold War; it was equally evidently not the case in others (such as the Balkans), where some states not only failed to offer protection to their citizens but actively threatened sections of the population. This led to two important shifts in how security was perceived.

The first of these was reflected in arguments in the UNDP 1994 'Human Development Report' in favour of the notion of 'human security', which could be defined as a freedom from threats in seven areas: providing economic security; food security; health security; environmental security; personal security; community security; and political security. The fifth, sixth, and (particularly) the seventh of these are all issues where states could actively either support or act against the rights of individuals, and should be addressed as key elements of an SSR programme. The others are all key development challenges, some of which can be addressed at a national level but many of which (and in particular health and environment security) need to be addressed globally.

The second shift was the recognition that, although the nation state remained the key concept in the political organization of the world, there could be occasions when a state was manifestly not fulfilling its responsibilities to its citizens—and in some cases was actually setting out to harm certain elements of the population. This became an area of particular concern after the Rwandan genocide of 1994 and Srebenica in 1995, in which the international community failed to intervene, raising questions about its 'responsibility to protect' (or 'R2P'). The emerging doctrine was set out in the UN Secretary General's Report of January 2009 'Implementing the Responsibility to Protect', which has three pillars:

- A state has a responsibility to protect its population from genocide, war crimes, crimes against humanity, and ethnic cleansing;
- The international community has a responsibility to assist the state to fulfil that responsibility;

- If the state manifestly fails to protect its citizens from mass atrocities, and peaceful measures have failed, the international community has the responsibility to intervene through coercive measures such as economic sanctions. Military intervention is considered the last resort.

The UN Security Council has the primary role in monitoring the first of these pillars; and only the Security Council can decide to proceed with military intervention in pursuit of the third pillar.

Technical Assistance (Technical Cooperation)

'Technical Assistance' or 'Technical Cooperation' is the provision of expertise, advice, or personnel in support of development objectives. Under the Marshall Plan following World War Two this involved the transfer of skills and advice into Europe from North America, and the training of Europeans in North America. Similar arrangements were put in place in the lead up to and following the transfer of colonial power to the newly independent countries of Asia and Africa. The challenge was that key institutions and structures—such as the judicial, civil service, education and health systems—were essentially those of the colonial powers, with key positions being held by colonial officials. So it was unrealistic to expect that change could happen very quickly; it would take time if the transition were to be smooth and effective.

In many cases, that is exactly what happened. Within the United Kingdom a Department of Technical Cooperation was established (taking over some of the functions of the old Colonial Office) before being folded into the newly formed Ministry of Overseas Development at the end of the 1960s. At the same time, the British Council became closely involved in the process of choosing candidates and making scholarships available to bring people to the UK for training.

In the Commonwealth countries of East Africa, for example, hundreds of experts—judges, teachers, civil servants, scientists—were seconded into the national systems either as Technical Assistance Officers (with their salaries paid in full by the British Government) or as Supplementees (with their costs supplemented by the British Government, and thus shared). The intention was that these officers would work alongside their local counterparts, training them and developing their skills over time until they were in a position to carry out the role fully and effectively. These schemes were also referred to as 'manpower aid'.

This largely worked (though it was an expensive model because of the costs of salaries, housing for experts and their families, school fees, home passages, tools of the trade, and so on). Over time, those British experts took on fewer line management responsibilities and moved increasingly into supporting, more specialized roles. These were often scientific or technical, and a number of specialized agencies were created within the UK both to provide and support those experts. The clue is in the name—the Natural Resources Institute; the Centre for Overseas Pest Research; the Tropical Products Institute. By the early 1990s, financial support for the last British judge who was integrated into the Kenyan judicial system had come to an end, and technical support was being provided in more specialized fields like forest and wildlife management systems.

As in other areas, the Cold War made its mark on technical cooperation, in particular through the scholarship programmes. Depending on which country they came from, and the political persuasion of its leaders, officials and specialists went in their thousands for training in Moscow, London, or Washington DC. Although those cities and capitals continue to have specialist institutions with relevant expertise, in recent years countries in Africa have looked increasingly to countries like China, India and Brazil for advice and technical support. They are seen as having recently gone through—and are still going through—some of the same development steps and therefore have more relevant and direct experience to share. There are now many Indian academics working in African higher and further education institutions. And there are other strong links between some of those countries, for example Brazil and the Lusophone countries of Africa such as Angola and Mozambique, which share a common language and elements of a common colonial history. This type of 'South–South' cooperation will undoubtedly increase.

There are also some interesting experiments in 'trilateral cooperation', where a traditional donor enables the sharing of the successful experience of one aid recipient to benefit another. For example, a hospital management programme in Sri Lanka, supported by Japanese aid, was replicated in Tanzania, with Sri Lankan experts rolling out the model in Tanzanian hospitals, with Japanese financial support. The lessons were then shared across Tanzania regionally, again with Japanese financial support. This is a logical direction of travel in an increasingly globalized world where the distinctions between 'developed' and 'developing' become less important, and common interest and the importance of transferrable skills development become more so.

Trade and the World Trade Organization (WTO)

The route from poverty to prosperity is often through trade, whether the country in question is South Korea, Mauritius, or the United Kingdom. It should come as no surprise, therefore, that there were plans to create an International Trade Organization (ITO) as a UN Specialized Agency in the mid-1940s to complement the activities of the so-called Bretton Woods Institutions, the IMF and World Bank. The Convention was never ratified, however, perhaps in part because along-side issues such as trade barriers and commodity agreements it was to be given authority to address sensitive areas like employment.

As an interim measure, the General Agreement on Tariffs and Trade (GATT) was agreed. 'Interim' was a relative concept; in practice the GATT survived for nearly half a century as a semi-institutionalized body, with the overall objective of focusing on the special needs of the developing countries and advocating for their increased participation in the global trading system. It was intended to pay particular attention to tariff barriers—the charges made to allow goods into better-off countries, which could discriminate disproportionately against exports from the poorest countries—but as various 'rounds' of discussion proceeded it inevitably became drawn into other areas too.

The 'Uruguay Round' lasted from 1986 to 1994. This opened up a whole panoply of new issues for discussion alongside tariffs, including non-tariff barriers, trade in services, intellectual property rights, and—issues which a number of member states felt fell outside the GATT mandate—trade in agriculture and textiles. The Uruguay Round concluded with the Marrakesh Agreement of April 1994. That Agreement also heralded the creation of the World Trade Organization (WTO), formally established on 1 January 1995, replacing the GATT as the legal and institutional foundation of the multilateral trading system of member countries. It sets out the principal contractual obligations determining how governments frame and implement domestic trade legislation and regulations, and is also the platform on which trade relations among countries evolve through collective debate and negotiation.

In practice, the WTO has had a difficult history. The 'Singapore Round' which succeeded the Uruguay Round ran into major difficulties over agricultural subsidies. 'The Doha Round'—specifically identified as a 'development round', with a specific focus on addressing the needs of developing countries—began in 2001, and had an original deadline of 2005 for agreement. But apparently intractable difficulties in particular over agricultural trade in commodities like cotton have meant that the round remains incomplete. This reflects the difficulty of getting agreement in a body where decisions are made by consensus, so that the withholding of agreement by a single country can block progress.

The difficulties of reaching agreement in the WTO are not so much over principles but over practice. Everyone agrees that in principle it should be possible for products such as textiles to be imported from least developed countries into developed countries without excessive charges being levied—but when do the quantities involved amount to 'dumping'? Everyone agrees on the importance of food safety rules, including inspection, labelling, and assurances of animal and plant health—so-called sanitary and phytosanitary measures—but standards will normally be higher and more affordable in better-off countries; how long should developing countries be given to reach those standards? Everyone agrees that there should be 'rules of origin' to determine whether products are actually produced in countries which stand to benefit from lower tariffs; but agreeing on harmonized rules is notoriously difficult in a globalized world where component parts of a complex piece of equipment are likely to come from many different countries.

The WTO can at least record one victory, however, which is over trade facilitation. This should have been non-controversial, and involves a $1 trillion package of reforms to global customs rules and the ease of transporting goods across national borders. A package of measures was agreed in early 2014, but India declined to ratify the package because of difficulties with the US on other trade issues. Failure to reach an agreement would have had catastrophic consequences for of many of the least developed countries, and ultimately the US and India made progress in resolving the other issues between them which meant that the Trade Facilitation Agreement was ratified at the end of 2014.

It remains to be seen whether agreement on issues other than trade facilitation can be reached as part of the Doha Round, or whether there will be a shift towards bilateral and regional agreements if the challenges of turning shared principles into shared practice at a global level become simply too difficult to manage. We shall see; one of the key Conferences in 2015 will be the WTO Ministerial meeting to be held in Nairobi from 15 to 18 December. In any event, it is clear that— to quote from the European Commission Communication of 2 June 2014[1] which was designed to feed into the Sustainable Development Goal process—'The role of trade and trade openness in the context of sound domestic policies and reforms is central to poverty eradication and sustainable development'.

Note

1. 'A decent life for all: from vision to collective action' (COM (2014) 335).

United Nations Development System

The United Nations was established on 24 October 1945. It followed a number of earlier mechanisms to promote peace and regulate conflict, such as the International Committee of the Red Cross (ICRC) and the Hague Conventions of 1899 and 1907. The League of Nations was established in 1919 by the Paris Peace Conference following the First World War, but proved to be largely ineffective, though some of the international structures created by the League (such as the bodies regulating aviation and post and telecommunications) were later absorbed into the structures of the United Nations.

The key role of the UN was defined as being to promote peace and resolve disputes, and the primary organ was the Security Council, comprising five permanent members (the P5—the United States, the Soviet Union, China, France, and the United Kingdom) and other members elected on a rotating basis. The ideological divisions of the Cold War meant that the UN's peacekeeping operations were severely hampered and had limited effect; one consequence of this—and the large number of joining states from Africa and elsewhere in the developing world—was a stronger focus on social and economic development.

This focus gave a more prominent role to the UN General Assembly and the Economic and Social Council (ECOSOC), which had the primary responsibility for delivering on the UN Charter mandate 'to achieve international co-operation in solving international problems of an economic, cultural, or humanitarian character'. The United Nations Development Programme (UNDP) was established in 1966 to rationalize the activities of the Expanded Programme of Technical Assistance (EPTA) and the UN Special Fund, to provide grant-based technical assistance, and to oversee the activities of a number of UN funds and programmes created at the end of the Second World War, or in the following few years, that focused on particular pressing issues.

Many of these funds and programmes were designed primarily to address long-term development issues. These included, for example, the United Nations Children's Fund (UNICEF), which was created in the first instance to aid European children after the War and subsequently took on a global mission, including upholding the Convention on the Rights of the Child; the UN Fund for Population Activities (UNFPA); and the UN Environment Programme (UNEP). Others such as the World Food Programme (WFP) and the United Nations High Commissioner for Refugees (UNHCR) focus more on emergency and humanitarian assistance.

The Funds and Programmes are responsible to the UN General Assembly (UNGA). There is another group of 'Specialized Agencies', which are autonomous organizations including, for example, the World Health Organization (WHO), which focuses on international health issues and disease eradication; the United Nations Educational, Scientific and Cultural Organization (UNESCO); and the Food and Agriculture Organization (FAO), which was established to support agricultural development and food security.

Even under the most auspicious of circumstances, the Secretary-General would have a complex enough task in bringing together and rationalizing the activities of the UN, touching as they do such a diverse range of issues as peace and security, justice and human rights, long-term development assistance, and short-term responses to disasters and emergency humanitarian crises. But in fact it is made very much more complicated because the specialized agencies are funded independently and responsible to their own boards (though their activities are in theory coordinated through ECOSOC), and even the UN's own funds and programmes are largely autonomous.

A first effort was made to reform the system (or at least the development elements of it) in 1969, through the 'Study of the Capacity of the United Nations Development System', which sought to strengthen the role of the UNDP in UN support for development cooperation, both in New York through the Administrator of UNDP and through resident representatives in the field. It failed, not because of the quality of the report, which was logical and convincing, but because the specialized agencies wanted to 'own' and manage their own technical assistance programmes.

It is unsurprising, perhaps, that reform of the peace and security elements of the system should have made no progress during the Cold War period, when the UN was accused regularly of favouring East or West by those on the other side of the ideological divide. Even when the distractions of the Cold War had come to an end, progress was limited—though the establishment in 1998 of the International Criminal Court (ICC), on which the Security Council can call, represented a step in the right direction. Entrenched interests meant that there was little progress in response to a panel established in 2000 to review the UN's peace and security activities or the 2003 panel focusing on 'Threats, Challenges and Change' which presented its Report *A More Secure World, Our Shared Responsibility* in 2003. And an attempt to integrate a set of reforms for UN procedures and structures into the World Summit in September 2005 (held in succession to the Millennium Summit) met with limited success.

Calls for reform of the development elements of the UN system made some progress in the early part of the 1990s (backed in some cases by a withholding of funds by governments to one or two of the specialized agencies like UNESCO). In 1994 the Office of Internal Oversight Services (OIOS) was created by the UN General Assembly to serve as an efficiency watchdog, and in 1997 the United Nations Development Group (UNDG) was created to maximize synergies and minimize overlaps between the thirty-two specialized agencies, programmes, and funds working on international development issues. The UNDG is chaired by the Administrator (Head) of UNDP; members of the Executive Committee also include UNICEF, WFP, and UNFPA.

The World Bank (see separate entry on the IFIs) is an independent specialized agency of the UN and is an observer at the UNDG, in an effort to bring closer coordination between the UN and the Washington-based institutions. These arrangements are also reflected in the field, where the coordination is the responsibility of a UN resident coordinator—often the head of the UNDP Office but sometimes, with

UNDP agreement, from other agencies. This takes a nod in the direction of—though ultimately falls short of—the recommendations of the 1969 'Capacity Study' already noted. The UNDG was reinforced in 2006 under the rubric of 'delivering as one', designed to strengthen the integration of the UN development system. This bolstered the notion of the UNDP as *primus inter pares*. It is worth noting too that the UN has made efforts to build closer partnerships with the private sector in its international development activities through the creation of the 'Global Compact' in 2000.

In his major work on the UN,[1] historian Paul Kennedy concludes that 'when all its aspects are considered, the UN has brought great benefits to our generation and...will bring benefits to our children's and grandchildren's generations as well'. This is a balanced and reasonable conclusion—though, to ensure that that happens, some serious institutional restructuring needs to take place to ensure that the global realities of current economic and political power are more accurately reflected in the make up of UN systems and structures. There is otherwise a danger that emerging powers will work around it rather than with it, and Paul Kennedy's prediction will be proved overoptimistic. The election of a new UN Secretary-General will take place at the end of 2016; history suggests that (as with new national governments) the opportunity for sweeping institutional change will be most evident in the first six months of the 'honeymoon' period of a new UNSG assuming office.

Note

1. Paul Kennedy, *The Parliament of Man: The Past, Present and Future of the United Nations* (New York: Random House, 2006), p. 290.

Recommendations for further reading

Much of the factual information in this section is readily available on the UN website <www.un.org>. Other useful background reading includes:

Stephen Browne and Thomas G. Weiss (eds), *Post-2015 UN Development: Making Change Happen?* (Abingdon: Routledge, 2014).

Linda Fasulo, *An Insider's Guide to the UN* (New Haven, CT: Yale University Press, 2004).

Jacques Fomerand, *The A to Z of the United Nations* (Lanham, MD: Scarecrow Press, 2009).

Mark Malloch-Brown, *The Unfinished Global Revolution: The Pursuit of a New International Politics* (New York: Penguin Press, 2011).

Adam Roberts and Benedict Kingsbury (eds), *United Nations, Divided World: The UN's Roles in International Relations* (2nd edn, Oxford: Oxford University Press, 1993).

Thomas G. Weiss and Sam Daws (eds), *The Oxford Handbook on the United Nations* (Oxford: Oxford University Press 2007).

INDEX

References to Notes will be followed by the letter 'n'